EVERYBODY
CHEATS

BY
NINA MANCUSO

Cover design: Robin Wilson
Interior design: Robin Wilson
Typography: Robin Wilson

Everybody Cheats
ISBN: 978-0692454329

Distributed to the trade by Createspace.com.

INTRODUCTION

I've never been lucky in love. I've made many poor decisions when it comes to dating, probably because I never truly loved myself. I guess I figured that if I dated guys who had no ambition or goals, then the inevitable breakup wouldn't hurt nearly as bad. I was right, but because of that idiotic thinking, I can't say that I've actually had a true heartbreak. I've been angry, bitter, and quite a bit traumatized, but not sure if I had my heart broken. I've never dated a guy good enough that could break my heart.

I went from being the ugly, hopeless romantic to the strong, independent woman who trusted no man and focused only on her career. And here I am now: A happy, strong, independent woman who has more compassion for animals and orphans than I can handle. I finally have my emotional, loving, motherly side back, and it feels wonderful.

That said, here is a brief history of my terrible choices and how they shaped my thinking about love.

The Bad Boy

The Bad Boy was my first boyfriend. I met him when I was depressed and had issues with cutting myself. I had a trying childhood and my way of coping was to slit my wrists. On top of those issues, I felt worthless because there was not one guy in my high school who wanted to date me. So when I met the Bad Boy, I was thrilled just to get a boyfriend.

He was the typical bad boy. He was 18, had some tattoos, smoked cigarettes and dropped out of school.

He was all about hating the world and everybody in it. I enjoyed him because he was carefree and aggressive.

Little did I know that I was a rebound for him. He just ended his however long relationship with his previous girlfriend, and she was not too fond of him for moving on. When she found out about us, she relentlessly called him until he dumped me. He went back with her.

I was hurt because her tactic was to cut herself until he took her back. So when he decided that her issues were more important than me and my emotional issues, I was upset. I cried for a few months, but soon got over it. And although I was depressed and felt unworthy of ever being loved, I still had the hopeless romantic dream that I would meet a wonderful man, and that kept me going.

The Bad Boy taught me that the ex-girlfriend is a threat, but nothing to be too concerned about. I firmly believed that it was just bad luck for me, but not something that would be a consistent theme.

So as you can see, I was not off to a good start. Then there was the "Drunk Punk."

The Drunk Punk

When I first met the Drunk Punk, I was a happy camper. I was a sophomore in college, living free, drinking, and having a great time. I wasn't hurt or lonely, just happy. And then I met the Drunk Punk. The Drunk Punk was my first serious boyfriend. We dated for nine months when I was 19 and he was 26.

He was a bad boy punk. He was also an alcoholic. He would smash holes in the walls during his frequent drunken stupors. Our relationship was founded and sustained on sex. He was a mess, and I was a crazy 19-year-old girl. He was angry, jealous, and manipulative. When it came to conversations, we couldn't agree on anything. When it came to sex, we explored this world and beyond.

But then he kept talking about how much he loved his previous girlfriend. He would always tell me that if only he treated her better, he would be with her instead of me. One night, I asked him if he would rather stay inside with me or go outside to talk about his ex-girlfriend. He chose to go outside and talk about his ex-girlfriend. Hearing this upsetting answer led me up the stairs and into the bathroom. He came after me and I told him to leave me alone. As I walked out of the bathroom to head down the stairs, I looked behind me and saw him charging. I cleared about 12 steps and landed right on my ass. I'm still paying for that injury eight years later.

Now he didn't leave me for his ex, but his desire to be with her ultimately pushed me out the door. I felt hurt and stupid that I would date another guy that preferred his ex-girlfriend over me. I was angry, but happy to be free. I still had a sliver of hope that I would someday find a guy that wouldn't want his ex-girlfriend in general. My trust was not completely broken yet. I still had hope that I would find an amazing man and live happily ever after.

The Drunk Punk taught me that the ex-girlfriend can be a threat without her being in the picture. So not only could I get left because of an overbearing ex-girlfriend, but I can be left for an ex-girlfriend who wanted nothing to do with my current boyfriend. By this point, I assumed that I would recognize the signs of a broken hearted boy.

I was wrong.

The Tortured Boy

Then there was the Tortured Boy. I met him shortly after my previous relationship with the Drunk Punk. We clicked right off the bat, and he was always nice to me. He stood up for me when everyone else was being rude. I could tell that he really liked me, and I really liked him back. Little did I know that he was completely broken on the inside.

He was living back home in the suburbs while I was away at school. We had a summertime fling. I really enjoyed his company. I found him very attractive. I'm not sure why I did now, but at the time I probably just needed a rebound.

Well, this poor boy was a victim to a conniving ex-girlfriend. I was livid. I couldn't believe that every single guy I dated has left me, or wanted to leave me, for their ex-girlfriend. At this point, I was starting my junior year in college, so I decided that I won't get serious with another man again. I stuck to my guns and stayed single for four years.

During those four years I managed to get excellent grades, good partying in, and eventually a job as a content marketer in Chicago shortly after graduation. I focused all of my attention on enjoying college and being single. I was so angry that I used men. I used them for what I needed and when they wanted a relationship, I said no. I turned down every guy because I wanted to guarantee myself a career and a strong life, and I wasn't going to risk my future again for some guy who will probably leave me for an ex-girlfriend.

The Tortured Boy taught me that every man will leave me for an ex-girlfriend. I became so bitter that all I wanted was money, not romance.

At this point, I refused to let any man into my life. I stayed single for four years until I met the boy who saved me, the Sweet Boy.

The Sweet Boy

I met the Sweet Boy at a friend's funeral, but I didn't see him again until a year later. I was parked at my friend's house waiting for him to pick me up so we could go out to a bar. While I was waiting, I was debating between moving to Sicily and getting hired at the software company. I didn't know if I would get hired, so I started making plans to move to Sicily for a year. Then my friend picked me up with the Sweet Boy in the car. I was still bitter and angry and I wanted to move to Sicily, not only because I'm Sicilian and I loved being there during my field school, but because I had no hope for American men.

But then the Sweet Boy started a conversation. We ended up dating for two years, and he was the nicest guy I've ever dated. He was super cute and smart, but he had no idea how to be a boyfriend and I was awful at being a girlfriend. Although I felt at times that I wasted two years of my life, I finally realize that had it not been for him, I would be a mess.

He saved me. He showed me that not every guy will leave me for his ex-girlfriend. He understood my pain and paranoia, and he was patient with me. He wanted me to feel OK. He wanted me to understand that just because I've been hurt in the past, doesn't mean that it's my destiny to be alone. He brought out my compassion.

Although he was the best boyfriend I've had to this point, we still had our issues. He never once sent me a text message, I always started the conversation. He never called me just to see how I was doing. Never! I still don't know what it's like to date a guy that actually cares about my well-being.

Overall, this relationship ended because I made the move to Nashville. He ended up dumping me a week before my journey.

But because of him, I learned that it isn't the ex-girlfriend that is a threat. It's my approach to a relationship with the thought that the ex-girlfriend is a threat.

I didn't know that he saved me until I was in Nashville and I started dating the Delusional Boy.

The Delusional Boy
Oh was this boy a mess. I met the Delusional Boy shortly after my move to Nashville. We immediately had an attraction to each other. I was in no way ready for a relationship since my previous one just ended a month before, but I was ready for a good lay. I loved the Sweet Boy,

but the sex was boring. So the Delusional Boy, sexually, was everything I wanted and needed. He was aggressive, in control, and hot. He was a foreigner, so bonus points. He was a great lay, but an awful human being.

But it was because of the Delusional Boy that I realized how the Sweet Boy saved me. The Delusional Boy was sitting on my couch and looking at his ex-girlfriend on Facebook. He looked at me and told me that she is the most beautiful girl in the world and that if he acted differently, they would still be together. I felt nothing. I didn't feel angry, hurt, or sad. Instead, I felt myself completely detached from the idea of us having a relationship. I was still there for the Delusional Boy emotionally. I still listened to him and tried to help him through his issues, but the idea of a relationship was taken off the table, and I wasn't in the least bit angry.

I then found myself crying in the shower. It hit me that it was because of the Sweet Boy that I didn't care about this issue anymore. It was because of his patience and love that I no longer felt bitter or angry. It didn't bother me in the least. I was still able to be compassionate towards the Delusional Boy without being angry that he had feelings for his ex-girlfriend.

Ultimately, this relationship ended because he was delusional. He yelled at me for things I've never done. He blamed me for all of his problems. He even tried the whole "I'm going to tear you down and rebuild you to be reliant on me" tactic. He wanted me to stay with him, but instead of being a good person, he tried to get me to lose myself and become what he wanted.

The Delusional Boy helped me realize a few things. First is that the ex-girlfriend issue no longer bothers me. Even more importantly, I realized that I shouldn't go for the mentally unstable. As women, we always want to fix men. We think it's cute that they need us to help them. Don't believe me? Look at that Christan Grey character. He is a complete mess, but Anastasia wanted to fix him. I actually don't know how that turns out because the book and movie were awful, but look at the message. It's a girl who wants to show a man who can't love how to love. Most of the time, it's a stressful process that isn't worth it in the end.

And Now I'm Here
I finally have an understanding of the man that I want and deserve, and I figured that out by dating all of the wrong guys first. I believe that in your dating years, you meet all of the wrong people for the right reasons. We will have the relationships that seemed great in the beginning, but ultimately come to an end. But each relationship is meant to help us understand the qualities that we desire in a spouse.

I now have a perfect image of the man I want and deserve. Physically, he is tall, preferably with dark hair and light eyes, and has a strong enough build to carry me around the house. He is mentally and financially stable (I've been a sugar momma for far too long). He is fun and silly, but also dominant. He is intelligent and takes pride in his work. He is caring, loving, and wants to be the protector. He also has a kinky side. An added bonus is a snappy dresser, who also has that bad boy side. Maybe a few tattoos here and there. Knowing my track record he is probably foreign. Of course, they probably only made one of these men, and I strongly believe that I will find him.

But I am able to have a clearly defined vision of the type of man I want because I acknowledged why all of my previous relationships failed. I not only looked at the beauties of my past relationships, but I also took the time to fully understand why each relationship didn't work in my favor.

Acknowledging a Breakup
Often-times, we dwell the end of a relationship more so than trying to understand why it didn't work. Acknowledging the reasons behind a breakup is truly the best way to grow as a person.

Let's take a look at some examples. The Bad Boy and I didn't work because the sanity of his ex-girlfriend was higher priority than his current girlfriend. The Drunk Punk and I weren't right for each other because we just didn't get along. The sex was great but that was it. The Tortured Boy and I weren't good for each other because he was too strung out on his ex-girlfriend. The Sweet Boy and I didn't work because we weren't sexually compatible. The sex was OK, but he wasn't a naturally dominant person, and I wasn't going to force him to be that way. And finally, The Delusional Boy and I were wrong for each other because he tried to control me.

When a relationship ends, we must look at what we learned and why the relationship didn't work. Every person we decide to date teaches us a lesson. It's essential that we understand and appreciate those lessons and apply them to ourselves and our future relationships.

Unfortunately, relationships are no longer taken seriously. Divorce is commonplace, and cheating has become not only acceptable, but encouraged. I want to help society. As much as I would love to lie back and watch our morals dissipate from this planet, I feel like I should be more constructive and help us try to salvage some morality. I want to explore the basics of relationships, the evolution of cheating and how that affects our society in a more detrimental way than most believe. I also want to revisit the advantages of being single, and suggest that our perfect person does exist, but we must be the best versions of ourselves if we ever hope to find our soulmate.

So, let's get started.

PART 1: EVERYBODY CHEATS

There are multiple articles floating around the internet asserting that cheating can strengthen romantic relationships. In reality, there's no legitimate reason to cheat on a partner. If you or your partner have cheated or are thinking about it, then you committed to the wrong person for the wrong reasons. We wouldn't cheat if we knew how to embrace our single years. We can find our soulmate if we listen to our inner voices and live our lives instead of seeking love.

But we're a society that cares more about finding that special someone over finding our way in life. We cherish the idea of relationships instead of our future. We all have a deeply rooted desire to find that perfect someone. But we can't find that perfect person if we don't know who we are and what we want. We can't find love if we want it for the wrong reasons, and wanting love for the wrong reasons leads to cheating.

As humans, we want someone there to help us through life. We want a partner in crime. We want someone to love us, to validate us, and to make us feel more wanted than we would ever feel alone. We want someone to prove to us that another human being can value us. Why do you think online dating sites not only exist but are highly successful? Last year, the US dating market was estimated to be worth about $2.2 billion, with average users spending about $239 per year on memberships.[1] These sites do so well because no matter who we are, we all have that desire to love. We may not want the typical house with the picket fence, the children, and the dog, but we all want to find that special someone. The truth is, our soulmate is out there, but most of us won't find them.

We won't find our soulmate because we settle. We are a dependent group of people that struggle to survive on our own. We commit for the wrong reasons, and often our relationships end because of a straying partner. We don't take marriage seriously. We think that building a family is a decision that has no consequences.

The root of cheating, I believe, stems from the fear of being single. We're so afraid of being with our own thoughts that we take any partner who is willing to stand by our side. If we can't be single, we commit because we're dependent and filling a void. If we're filling a void, we cheat.

Relationships are meant to be meaningful. We should commit to a person that we can, in some way, envision marrying. That said, all excuses we give for cheating on our partner are invalid. We wouldn't cheat if we knew how to be single. If we ever hope to find that perfect person, we can't keep settling. We need to learn how to stand on our own. We're only cheating ourselves if we refuse to do so.

To find our soulmates, we must build a foundation during our single years. We must embrace our time alone in order to find and truly appreciate a wonderful partner. We can have fulfilling relationships. We can have love at first sight. We just need to know who we are so we can recognize our one true love.

We need to change our current dating trend.

In today's world, many relationships fail because of a cheating partner. We cheat during our younger years, and we cheat on our spouses. Cheating knows no age, gender or social status. What's worse is that cheating has become expected. If we're the cheater, we justify our actions with some stupid excuses. If someone cheats on us, we're not as surprised as we should be. We no longer view relationships as a sacred bond between two people. We see relationships as a time-filler. Relationships fill our voids until they fall apart due to an unstable foundation.

We have unstable foundations because romance is no longer the norm for society. We don't have those long phone conversations with our love interests. Do you even remember the last time you debated over who should hang up first? We don't find any excitement in surprising our partner. We don't talk, we text and we Facebook message. We no longer expect to meet our soulmate during our daily activities and errands. Instead, we browse Tinder to find someone to partake in a sexual excursion. That romance that is almost gone from society has taken its toll, and it has led to cheating.

For the record, both sexes do cheat. Women tend to cheat for emotional stability. Men usually cheat because they commit to the wrong people for the wrong reasons. And they think with their penises. Some men just cheat because they can. For men, instead of releasing the Kraken with a breakup, they would rather cheat to satisfy their needs. But no matter why we cheat, we brought our poor behavior upon ourselves. We can't blame anyone else for the path we choose to take. We don't cheat because our partner provoked us in some way. We cheat because we got stuck in a situation that we refuse to leave.

Whether we cheat because we're bored or we want the thrill, there's no valid excuse for cheating. The real reason we cheat is because we're co-dependent, entitled, and we have no idea when we should commit to someone. The truth is: We wouldn't cheat if we enjoyed our single years.

But since we don't value the years where we flower into an adult, we cheat. We cheat because we can, because the sex is boring, or sometimes for revenge. We cheat because we feel stuck in our current relationship, or because we want to see what else is out there. These are not valid reasons for cheating. These are all just petty excuses for bad behavior.

1. THEORIES FOR CHEATING

The strongest theory for cheating is that it's in our nature as humans to cheat. Multiple people say that as humans, we're not meant to be monogamous. These theories need to be inspected further. These theories are more against monogamy than they are for cheating, but these theories also justify our cheating behavior. According to some writers, there are multiple reasons as to why we're awful at monogamy. I don't believe that any of these ideas can be considered theories.[2]

The "bodies are meant for multiple partners" theory
This theory basically states that penises are shaped to flush out other men's sperm. For women, our bodies have multiple orgasms, so we must always have multiple partners. Finally, we make noises when we fuck, and those noises are mating calls.

I don't doubt that penises are shaped for that function and that women's vaginas are meant to have multiple orgasms. I do doubt that these are valid theories against monogamy. Clearly, the penis and vagina are meant to give pleasure to both sexes. The noises let our partners know that they're doing a wonderful job. Most people enjoy making their partner scream because it boosts their egos turns them on. I doubt the man is thinking *"I love her screams because it means she wants dozens of other men to come here and fuck her better than I do."* I'm sure that gets some people off, but probably not everyone.

The "our ancestors didn't have monogamy so it must be nature to cheat" theory

This theory tells us that because our cavemen ancestors lived in hunter-gatherer tribes and didn't have one sole partner means that we shouldn't be monogamous. Because our hunter-gatherer ancestors shared resources and partners, and because everyone raised the children in the tribe, that means we should be the same way. This theory also suggests that one of our closest primate relatives, the bonobo monkeys, has constant sex with multiple partners, so that means that it's our nature to do the same.

For starters, hunter-gatherer tribes were much smaller than our average society. There are still hunter-gatherer tribes living in South America and New Zealand, and they probably act the same as our hunter-gatherer ancestors. However, we don't live in hunter-gatherer tribes. We live in a society with millions of people. Most of the world is civilized and we have one too many children in orphanages because too many people who aren't prepared for children have them. This theory is silly because it wouldn't work for a country with 318 million people.

When a society settles, they have smaller family units. These family units now contain two parents raising and supporting their children. It's completely reckless to have children with multiple people when we can't even support our already overflowing foster system.

As for the bonobo monkeys, they aren't responsible for paying rent, medical bills, school and basic necessities for their children. Bonobo monkeys have everything they need in that forest. What else are they going to do besides eat and fuck all day? They may be our closest primate relative, but we are still two different species. Plus, titi monkeys are monogamous and much cuter overall.

The "sexual passion fades" theory

This theory basically states that after the honeymoon phase, the sexual desire for one another fades. And the only way to reignite that spark is to cheat on our partners.

If we use our single years and sleep with as many people as we want, we'll find a partner to sexually satisfy us for the rest of our lives. The problem is that most of us hate the thought of being single so much that we jump from relationship to relationship. We don't ever take the time to explore the world and what's out there. It all comes back to the fact that once we take the time to know who we truly are and what we want, we will find the person who elevates us for the remainder of our lives.

I believe, and call me a hopeless romantic if you must, that there is one perfect person for everyone. There is one person out there who will understand me in and out, and that sexual passion will never fade. We have drifted so far from the idea of true love that we basically accept the fact that we won't ever meet someone who is perfect for us, so we settle and that sexual passion fades. However, if we take that time to explore and try to understand our purpose in this life, we will find the perfect person and experience true love. Or so I hope.

The "we need variety" theory

This theory states that our brains are wired to want variety. Therefore, it isn't our fault that we sleep around because it's what our brains dictate.

Yeah, and we can enjoy the variety during our single years. It's all about timing here. When you're single, you get to taste anyone from anywhere. Get that out of your system during your free years and you won't want variety nearly as much after you get married. But, if you're a serial dater and you constantly need to be in a relationship, then you'll crave more variety and cheat.

Society Rallies against Monogamy

In recent years, the case against monogamy has been relentless. Every five minutes there's a new article describing why we're not meant to be monogamous. Some even suggest that we're naturally polygamous creatures.

There was a time when polygamy worked for humans. But we have evolved. We have grown from small bands to overpopulated societies. The only time a polygamous relationship will work in the Western World is if you join a commune.

Don't believe me? Then I challenge you to try being with three different partners and all three of your partners must be aware of the other two partners. So, if you're a woman, have three boyfriends and they all must know about each other. If you're a man, have three different girlfriends, and they all must know about each other. If you're gay, try it out with whatever sex it is that you desire.

The point here is that your three partners will probably all have Facebook and Instagram. We're too selfish to share, and I can't image three socialized women being okay with sharing one man. I say socialized because it doesn't count if you live in Utah. Those women are born and raised to be sister wives, we're not.

We became monogamous for a reason. Society grew too large and we needed smaller family units to raise our children. Unless we all decide to join communes, monogamy works. It's called adapting to the world around us.

2. SOCIETY JUSTIFIES CHEATING

We're in a time where bloggers are promoting cheating as a natural instinct and not a dishonorable action. Instead of taking responsibility for the fact that we hurt another person, we justify our actions by saying that we are naturally polygamous and our basic human need is to have sex with as many people as possible. It's unnatural for us to be with one person for the rest of our lives, so we're supposed to cheat. Cheating on our partners is selfish, rude, childish and unacceptable. If you cheat on your partner, you're probably not a good person. Accept that you're not a great person and change if you desire, but don't claim that cheating is the right thing to do because you think it is.

Justifying Our Cheating Behavior

Justifying bad behavior is one of the worst things we can do as a society. Instead of saying *"Oh, I fucked up, I'm sorry and I promise to learn from this mistake"* we say *"well my actions were fully warranted!"* It's no surprise that we tend to justify our bad behavior. Instead of taking responsibility for our actions, we make up ridiculous reasons as to why our actions are correct. For example, if we cheated on our partner, we say we did so because they provoked us. Our partner either bored or annoyed us. We either want something more or maybe something less.

To demonstrate the absurdity that comes with justifying bad behavior, I'll be referencing an article that came across my Facebook feed. This article is called *Six Reasons to*

Cheat on Your Girlfriend.[3] This brilliant author first starts out by telling us that men shouldn't be ashamed of cheating because it's natural for them to cheat.

He first claims that men cheat because it's in their nature to spread their seed freely and without consequence.

Next, he continues to give us six "legitimate reasons" to cheat on our partners. This boy, and I say boy because clearly he isn't a man yet, lists six reasons as to why his cheating behavior is acceptable. And not only is this fucktard saying that cheating is acceptable, but he's encouraging his readers to cheat.

Yes, if we haven't evolved since we became a human species. Chimps are in constant competition to impregnate as many females as possible so that he can then become the alpha male. Well, I understand that we are closely related to chimps, but does that mean we still act like them?

"Thousands of years ago men spread his seed freely." Right, and then we evolved. Does this guy really expect us to act the same way that we did when we were evolving? Do you really think Mother Nature created men just to impregnate women? If that was Mother Nature's intent then I'm sure that she thoroughly regrets that decision today. We are way too overpopulated. We have over 400,000 children in orphanages, and that's just in America. We have more children who have mothers, but no fathers. So, if we really want to listen to this guy then that means that all men should go impregnate women. They shouldn't raise the child. They should just impregnate the women. That's encouraging.

Secondly, he suggests cheating to "improve your game."

Well, you can hit on women while you're single. This point is complete nonsense. You have plenty of time to improve your game while you're single. There is no point in committing to someone if you simply plan to cheat. Did everyone forget what the fuck a commitment is?

He then suggests cheating as a solution for your girlfriend cheating on you, and she cheats because women only want men for stability reasons.

If you're dating a woman that you think is only with you for stability, then you should probably dump her, and be single. Why does everyone have such an issue with being single?

And when I thought his reasons couldn't get worse, they did. His fourth reason to cheat on your girlfriend is because you can get away with it. I wish I were lying.

This reason is completely stupid. If you're doing something simply because you can get away with it, then you may need to lead a slightly more interesting life. Go visit a waterfall or something. I am sure there are other things you can do to occupy your time than disrespecting not only a commitment, but another person.

His fifth reason is because cheating will improve your relationship.

This idea is utterly stupid, and I cannot believe this article has been published and shared, on the internet. Unless you're in an open relationship, cheating will more than likely destroy the relationship. If you're sexually bored with your partner, then you're with the wrong person. Some people are kinky, and some are bland and boring. If you're bored in your sex life, then that person isn't the right one for you. And trust me, there are a lot of kinky people out there, and there is one especially for you. If your partner isn't that person, then don't be afraid to be single, breakup. That way you don't have to cheat. You can be single and fucking a bunch of bitches on your business trip. Once again, you should just be single.

Finally, his sixth reason to cheat on your partner is because it will teach you how to live on the edge by forcing you to rotate phone and Internet passwords.

Constantly rotating the password on your phone, limiting the use of your camera, clearing your history, getting tested regularly and having a consistent story sounds unnecessary. I apologize, but I have real life problems and situations that I need to deal with, and I sure as fuck am not going to add being a sneaky little asshole to the list. I apologize, but intelligent people don't induce extra stress on themselves. Only those people who have no hobbies or morals enjoy these tedious and malevolent tasks. If you are one of those types of people, go fuck yourself.

So there you have it: One dipshit who is out to influence a bunch of other dipshits to act like complete and total dipshits. Really? Couldn't he have just been single? It seems like every reason he provided just points to the fact that he should be single. Maybe he should rename his article "Six Reasons to be Single."

3. EXCUSES, EXCUSES, EXCUSES

There are multiple excuses that we give for cheating. Sometimes it's because of the boring sex. Sometimes it's because our partner drives us nuts. Other times, we cheat just to cheat. But is it possible that we cheat because we don't know when to commit or when to exit a relationship? There is no excuse for cheating. But, since this is a book about everybody cheating, let's explore some pitiful excuses.

"Because I can"
Well just because you can doesn't mean you should. I don't think this needs much explanation. This is a horrible reason to cheat. I mean, unless you're aiming to win the Biggest Douche in the Universe Award (previously won by John Edward), I suggest that you don't cheat just because you can. It's a dick move. I'm sure you CAN jump off a bridge, but would you?

If you're a serial cheater, then stop dating. Don't bring another person into your web of bullshit. Don't continue to cheat for the thrill. That's just rude. If you're cheating because you can, then you must breakup. Don't cheat.

"The sex is boring"
If the sex was great in the beginning, then you two probably just need to spice things up. You did, however, make a poor decision if you committed to someone who wasn't good in bed from the start. Whatever your situation, unsatisfactory sex is not a reason to cheat, it's an excuse.

We've all slept with someone who couldn't figure it out. The poor performer shouldn't be called again. Not to be rude, but if you're looking for sex, then there's no point in sleeping with someone who doesn't do it right. I wouldn't waste your time, unless you have a thing for teaching people. If you commit to someone who doesn't flip your switch, you're going to have a bad time. You're going to have boring sex and you'll lose attraction to that person.

A lack of sexual compatibility is one of the main reasons people cheat. We all have different sexual needs. Some of us like the standard missionary position and others like to be a bit kinky. We can't have a successful relationship with someone who doesn't please us sexually. If you're a submissive woman and want an aggressive man in the bedroom, you can't make it last with someone who isn't naturally aggressive. You'll find yourself masturbating or cheating. You can't make a dominant girl submissive just as much as you can't make a submissive man dominant.

And if your partner doesn't like what you do, don't make them do it. Your partner shouldn't perform uncomfortable tasks just because it's what you want. Don't make anybody sign any contracts to have sex that frightens them. You two need to either be experimental and enjoy each others' kinkiness or you need to get out of the relationship. The same goes for a woman that doesn't like being roughed around in the bedroom. If your man is aggressive and you don't like it, you shouldn't put up with it for his sake. You should break up.

It's obvious that sex is incredibly important for a successful relationship. If the two of you feel like the passion is gone, there is a high chance that you committed to the wrong person. Or, it could also mean that you two haven't done the deed in a while and you should do so. But people cheat when they're bored in the bedroom.

My friend Cheryl cheated on her boyfriend, multiple times, before they broke up. Cheryl said she cheated because she didn't know how to end it. So, instead of confronting him about the lack of sexual excitement, she received it elsewhere and everywhere. Seriously, everywhere. She was fucking in the bathroom at my ex-boyfriend's house, in her bedroom, at the bar, on a porch. It was pretty impressive. But she stayed with him for six months before he dumped her. She had the problem of being in an unfulfilling relationship. Her solution was to cheat. My solution would be to end the relationship. If your partner isn't pleasing in bed now, they probably won't be later.

If you lost the spark, then go on a retreat. Watch some porn. Maybe you two just need to get excited again. But don't be irrational. Don't cheat.

But just because someone is really good in bed doesn't mean you should date them either. Often, relationships founded on sex fail because we don't see the other person's negative qualities until they get lazy in the bedroom. Things seem perfect when the sex is great, but don't be blinded by the sex. Don't stay with a horrible person because they're phenomenal in bed.

Trust me. You're soulmate will be a great person and even better in bed. We are humans. We have hands. We have an imagination. Go have sex with the person of your desire. You may not have the touch of another, but at least you get to touch yourself.

The point here is that if the sex is boring, we're with the wrong person. If we're with a person who fulfills us mentally and emotionally, then we've found a friend. Our soulmate satisfies all three needs. If you're not sexually pleased with your partner, then you must breakup. Don't cheat.

"My partner cheated on me, and I want revenge"

Just because someone hurts our feelings doesn't mean that we should act like them. Being cheated on is not a reason to cheat, it's an excuse. Take the high road and leave the person that cheated on you. Even if you're married, you're better off getting a divorce than cheating out of revenge. And if you have children, try to act your age and hold off on having a revenge cheating battle. That's absolutely ridiculous behavior.

I once knew a girl named Malory who was in such a relationship. She was bored with her boyfriend, got drunk and cheated on him. He found out and cheated on her back. The two of them stayed together for three years with constant fights and revenge sex battles. She would always complain about how he's an asshole that cheated on her. He constantly called her a bitch. They would fuck, make up and then fight again.

Now if that sounds like a good time, then go right ahead. The point is that it makes little sense to cheat on someone that cheated on you. If your partner betrays your trust, you must break up. Don't cheat.

"My partner bores me, mentally"

Well, if you can't have conversations with your partner, then you're clearly with the wrong person. You should have stimulating and engaging conversations with your partner. Mental compatibility is a good reason to date someone. Just because you chose a boring person to date isn't a reason to cheat, it's an excuse.

There's no reason to commit to someone who bores us. Let's think of the top reasons why people cheat; bored in the bedroom and bored in the relationship. If you're with a boring person, you're going to want to explore. You can't be with someone who hates the same music and movies you do. You can't be with someone that isn't interested in conversation. Communication is a big portion of a relationship. However, I do understand that sometimes we enter relationships for legal reasons. If you're bored in this type of relationship, that's more understandable. Essentially you were doing a favor for a foreigner, just like an old friend of mine.

I have an incredibly accomplished friend Karen who was married to an attractive man from Sweden. He looked perfect, as do most of the people from Sweden. He was sexy, had the accent and a hot body. Basically, any girl would love to jump on it. She loved him, in the beginning. They married to keep him in the States, but they also loved each other. But as the years went on, she got bored. But Karen was also a bit of a queen. She would order him around the house. She forced him into activities that he didn't want to do. She demanded a lot from him, but he could never do enough to satisfy her needs. During the summer before our senior year in college, she took her opportunity to head overseas for an internship.

Karen was working in Europe for some time, and during her stay she met this guy in Belgium. The two started talking, which eventually led to sex. She really liked the sex. She loved the sex so much that after she was back in the States, she took bi-monthly trips out to Belgium just to get some. She would tell her husband that she was flying out there for work reasons. I don't think he found out until she completely left him. But the problem was that she didn't want to give up her husband or her boy toy. So Karen stayed with her husband until she finished her schooling, then she officially left him to get a masters in Europe somewhere.

The point here is that Karen was mentally bored and therefore damaged two people in the process. Her solution to her mental boredom was to leave her husband for someone else. Her boy toy enjoyed the same movies, the same music and they loved doing the same activities. She loved caring for his children more than she enjoyed a demanding life in the States. But, of course her second relationship ended because she was too demanding.

In short, if you got yourself into a boring relationship with a boring person, then you must become an adult and break up. Don't cheat.

"But I'm stuck in this relationship"
In reality, we're never stuck in a relationship. We get stuck because we feel mentally defeated. But you need to get out of that slump and rise above it. I say this about abusive relationships, too. I understand that the law does very little to help victims of domestic violence, but there are ways and there are people that care. If you're in one of these situations, please seek help. No person deserves to be a victim of domestic violence.

But if you're not a victim of domestic violence, then you're not stuck in a relationship. You have complete control over your life. Being "stuck" in a relationship is still not a reason to cheat, it's an excuse. You're being lazy.

We choose who we get to be with. We don't live in a country where we have no choice over our partner. Unfortunately, I know such a person who is stuck in a relationship. Barry believes that he won't be able to find anyone else at his age. Barry isn't in love with his girlfriend, but he loves and cares for her. She has been asking for a ring for some time now, but he won't propose because he isn't sure if he wants to marry her. That should be his brightest sign but some people don't like to look. So instead they bought a house together. He still has no plans to propose, but he stays with her because it's comfortable and safe. And she has a history of cheating. Granted, I don't believe that either of them has cheated on each other, but if they continue their comfortable relationship, someone is going to break.

But there are plenty of people out there that do cheat because they feel stuck in a relationship. The truth is that if you made a poor choice and you feel stuck, then you must grow up and break up. Don't cheat.

"But I'm curious about what else is out there"
Then be single. You commit to someone because they intrigue you. Cheating on someone because you're curious about another person isn't a reason to cheat, it's an excuse.

There is this time frame when you're not with anybody. That's when you get to be curious and explore the other options out there. Being curious about what sex is like with a different person is a piss poor excuse to cheat. I'm curious about Germans in the bedroom, but I won't test that out if I'm committed to someone. No. I would go to Germany now and take a few test runs, get it out of my system. You get to have sex with anyone when you're single. You wouldn't have the curiosity if you fully utilized your single years. Basically, listen to Rita from Bridesmaids when she says, "That's why every girl needs those slutty college years. To experiment, get it out of your system. Find out what you like."

If you're really curious, then you must break up. Don't cheat.

4. SITUATIONS DESIGNED FOR CHEATING

Before we attempt to understand the scenarios where people are most likely to cheat, we must first confirm the fact that boys and girls will probably cheat. If you're a woman looking for a man, don't date a boy. Same goes for the men. If you're a man looking for a woman, don't date a girl.

But the problem here is that most people in our society are girls and boys. It seems like we've stopped evolving in recent years. We stopped learning from our mistakes and we're justifying our actions instead. We don't grow up. Being a man or being a woman is a maturity thing. If you're more mature than your partner, you may be with the wrong person. Now, remember, being silly and being immature are two totally different concepts. You can be a mature adult with a silly personality. Immature people are obviously just not mature.

That said, it's important that we first understand the difference between girls and women, boys and men.

The Difference between Boys and Men
Taylor Swift still struggles to figure out the difference. Boys are the ones that have no drive or path in life, like bad boys. Bad boys are good for fucking but horrible for dating. Unless he's a reformed bad boy, but I think only three of these exist on this planet. A man has his career in order. A man has his finances straight. A man has respect for women, especially his partner and his mother. A man wants to support his partner because he's proud of her. A man cherishes his relationship. A man chooses

a woman because he loves her and her quirks. A man is secure with himself. A man takes pride in the man he has become. A man is to the point about what he wants.

A boy, on the other hand, has no regards for your feelings. A boy doesn't have a career or maybe even a job. A boy isn't financially stable. A boy dates you because he likes having a girlfriend. A boy isn't proud of himself. A boy is afraid of the world and change. A boy is likely to play mind games because he isn't secure with himself. A boy is likely to cheat, but a real man isn't.

It's fine to date boys in your younger years. For instance, high school is a great time to date boys. College is a great time to play with boys. After college, you need to better your game so you can try to snag one of the few remaining men in our country.

You can't be a woman dating a boy and expect to have a truly fulfilling relationship.

The Difference between Girls and Women

Girls can be catty, vengeful and manipulative. Girls rely on others for their future. Girls are demanding and expect everything to be handed to them. And more often than not, girls will not stand and support their significant other for the sake of supporting them.

Women are secure with themselves. Women have their shit together. Women support their significant others. Women have their own stable foundation that they openly choose to share with their partners. Girls get what they want from people while women get what they want out of life. A girl is likely to cheat, but a real woman isn't.

And now that we understand the differences between girls, boys, women, and men, let's look at those scenarios we find ourselves in that eventually lead us to cheat.

The "I just got rich and I need to enjoy the options" scenario

This one is obvious. Just look at Hollywood. An actor makes it big, and soon he's snorting coke and banging every piece of ass across the globe. Someone who has just struck it rich and has a claim to fame shouldn't settle down. They need this time frame to enjoy the luxuries of having money.

If you meet a person and they just hit their claim to fame, whether it be as a promotion at work or on a larger scale, these people need to get the excitement and fun out before they settle down. If you try and date someone who just hit a high in their life, they need to enjoy that high before they can consider settling down. If you convince a person in this position to date you, be wary. You're new found love may cheat because they are still experiencing the glamorous life without consequence.

The "I have a lot of money and need a spouse" scenario

This scenario includes the elite people in our society who need to marry for publicity reasons. We see it all the time with politicians, and we know they cheat. But the marriage is more than likely founded on the need to look good in the public eye. This scenario leads to cheating because usually both partners understand that they're in it for the public image.

And you have to figure that if they lose money in the divorce, which is not likely since they probably signed a prenuptial agreement, they can move on easily. In short, if you're looking to marry someone who needs a spouse for the good looks, there's a high chance that your partner will stray.

The "I need a partner so I don't end up alone" scenario

This scenario includes the people who are terrified of being single. They are scared that if they find someone, that the person will leave. These people need to be married young so that they don't miss their window. The fearful stay with a person because they believe that they'll never find anyone else. They are destitute to be single forever if they don't find their partner now.

It doesn't matter if it's a turbulent relationship. What matters is that you found someone to tolerate, and they will do for a family. Unfortunately, you won't be able to tolerate that person for much longer. If you meet someone who needs a relationship to validate their lives, you need to run. I understand that it's tempting to want to heal people; but if someone is so scared that they're going to end up alone that they'll take anyone who offers, your relationship is headed for disaster. And because one or both partners need a relationship for validation, there's a high chance of finding someone else when the relationship gets boring.

The "cheating runs in my family" scenario

This scenario includes the people who were raised in a family where cheating was prevalent. These kids witnessed their family fall apart due to a cheating partner. This experience tends to go one of the two ways. Either the young adult refuses to cheat because they saw the effect it had on their parent or the young adult turns into a cheater, like their cheating parent or parents.

This scenario is prime for cheating because the child born in a cheating household tends to cheat because they were taught that it's OK. If you're dating someone who hasn't accepted and learned from their past, then they may cheat. Many of us believe that we're products of our childhood. But we aren't a product of our past. We have complete control over our lives and our actions. We are supposed to learn from our past, not be defined by it. It isn't what happens to you, but what you do with what happens to you.

The "I'm not sure if I'm over my ex" scenario

This is the ultimate "I'm going to cheat on you" scenario. Don't ever get involved with someone who misses their ex. They are not ready for a relationship and you don't want to be their second choice.

And for those in love with their exes, please, for the love of humanity, DO NOT COMMIT TO SOMEONE IF YOU ARE NOT OVER YOUR EX! You're wasting everybody's time. You're not ready for a new relationship, and a new relationship won't heal your wounds. Only learning from the relationship and spending time alone will do that. Instead of wasting your time on an old flame, spend that time trying to rebuild your own foundation.

Do you remember that boy I mentioned earlier named "The Tortured Boy"? Well, he's still heartbroken over his ex-girlfriend. She toyed with his mind and, 12 years later, he still isn't over her. He has wasted over a decade of his life on high hopes that his manipulative ex-girlfriend would come back to him. He spent 12 years waiting for that relationship to be right. That relationship is never going to be right or perfect because they aren't good for each other. But he is incapable of seeing through his delusional wishes. He will never be able to fully commit any part of himself to a new person because part of him is wishing that every girl is his ex-girlfriend.

This scenario includes the people not over their exes. These are the ones most likely to cheat on you with their ex. If they have any unresolved feelings for that person, you need to run. That said, if you're dating someone who recently got out of a relationship, be cautious. If they're consistently talking to or about their ex, it's best to run. This person will either leave you for their ex or they will be thinking about their ex the entire time they're with you. Go ahead and don't believe me. Watch it happen. And if they don't leave you for an ex, they will probably go back to them after your dating period fizzles out.

The "I've given up" scenario
This scenario includes the people that settle for something less than what they truly want. There is no such thing as "this person is good enough." There is someone out there that is perfect for you. Don't settle because you think you won't find them or deserve them. If you truly deserve to find your soulmate, you will. If you

settle, you'll be unhappy and probably end up cheating. Settling is the main reason people cheat and it gets much more air time later in this book.

The "I enjoy when my friends find me attractive" scenario
This scenario includes the boys and girls that want everyone to find them attractive. Dating someone who is currently at this stage in life is a bad idea. They just want to feel loved and pretty, and they will get that validation from anywhere and everywhere. People in this scenario also tend to be the compulsive liars.

I still can't believe the amount of effort that we invest into lying. Why in the world would you want to spend your hours manipulating your phone? Why would you want to spend the effort on maintaining lies? I never lie because I'm a bit forgetful. It's much less effort to tell the truth. Telling the truth is a great time saver too. But we enjoy wasting our time by being sneaky. If that's what you're into, why don't you try being a CIA agent?

I just don't get why this needs to be explained. You're expending an immense amount of effort into lying to someone. How immoral are we? Not only are we cheating, but we're taking time-consuming precautions to make sure that we get away with it. You are literally spending your hours tormenting another person, even if they don't know that you're cheating yet. Does it feel good to actively spend your time betraying the person you supposedly love?

PART 2: WHY WE REALLY CHEAT

As you can see, there are plenty of excuses and scenarios begging us to cheat, but they are just excuses for poor situations. The real reasons we cheat are because we lack morals and romance, and we don't respect ourselves or our partners. We don't care about other people, we just care about ourselves. We're dependent when we need someone there to make us feel wanted. We have no respect when we don't care that we hurt another person. We have no morals if we're willing to do anything to get our way. We have no romance when we stop dialing our partners when we have some free time to talk.

Then we end up settling. Settling is the main reason we cheat. Settling is the most dangerous game to play. Settling on good enough means you gave up. Settling is a weakness and is the death of all relationships. There's no excuse for settling. It's one thing to stay in a relationship in hopes of working it out, but if you know it's not going to work, you need to break up. We deserve someone who is perfect for us, not a complete compromise. No matter how bat shit crazy you are, there's someone out there equally as wacked out just for you, I promise.

So why do we really cheat?

5. BECAUSE WE LACK RESPECT AND MORALS

You wouldn't get into a relationship with someone that you don't respect. It's not even just about respecting that person; it's about respecting yourself and the relationship. You have to respect the commitment you made to someone. That person trusts you to be a good companion. You don't respect that person if you're willing to disrespect the commitment you made to each other.

We have no respect

This issue of respect goes far beyond romantic relationships. It seems like we don't respect anyone anymore. The lack of respect that we have for people is so outlandish that I'm going to divert from romantic relationships for a minute.

I'm going to mention Daniel Tosh. It really bothered me that he had to apologize for making a typical Daniel Tosh joke. For those unaware, he offended a female audience member during a stand-up show at the Laugh Factory in Hollywood. He was making rape jokes, as he does, and a woman was upset and decided to tell him that rape jokes aren't funny. In turn, he made a rape joke towards her suggesting that it would be funny if five guys raped her right there. Granted, not the best response, but in all fairness, she was being disrespectful. He is a comedian and it's impolite to interrupt a show. It's not only rude to the comedian, but beyond unfair to the audience. These people paid good money to see him perform these types of jokes. I'm sure heckling makes for some drama, but it's disrespectful. Would you shout at the actors performing the *Book of Mormon* if you didn't like something they said? I sure hope not.

The point is that we must respect ourselves and our choices. If we say we're going to commit to someone, you have to see that through. If everything inside of you is telling you to run, then run. Don't stay with someone and get what you need elsewhere. It's unnecessary betrayal.

We have no morals

Do we have morals? It seems like we're out for what we want and we don't care who gets in the way. The scary part is that we go to extensive lengths to prove how immoral we are. We have the insecure girls that hate when their exes move on. We have the people who reset passwords and rotate phone apps to avoid being caught cheating. We have groups of people that torment a lone wolf just to catch it and watch it die. Could you imagine what would happen if we put this much effort into being a good human being? We would have the world's best doctors, scientists, astronomers, you name it. We could be a society of accomplished people with fulfilling love lives. But do we put our effort towards school or finding ourselves? No.

We prefer to watch an outsider crumble. We prefer to get what we want regardless of who gets hurt in the process. We don't care about anyone else but ourselves.

We're dependent

Face it, when dependent people get bored with their current partner, and something better comes along, chances are there is sex with the new toy. Dependent people need someone there. If they're unsatisfied with their current partner, they stay with them because it's a safe option; but they cheat because what they really want is the new person. Dependent people struggle to be alone. Even if they don't have a partner, they always have friends with them. Introspection is the most frightening concept to a dependent person. Dependent people stay with their partner so that they always have someone there, but their inner desires are fulfilled by another person.

Dependency is a major reason why we have so many issues when it comes to cheating. No matter what excuse you give for cheating, it all comes down to the fact that you should've just been single. But since we are such a dependent group of people, we'll always resort to cheating. Rather than being single and alone, we would rather have someone there who isn't entirely right for us. Truth is, that right person can be at your doorstep, but you would never know it because you never took the time to figure out who you are yet.

Instead, we want someone there to hold us over until we find that right person. That's why we have so many cases of the ex, and so many serial daters.

The Case of the Ex
Then there are the dependent people who continuously get back together with their ex. It's almost like a game of cat and mouse, except with two stupid people of the same species. My question is this: Why in the hell would you be on again, off again with someone? I get that maybe the first time you both made a mistake. But, more than once is unacceptable. You should know by now how that

relationship is going to turn out. This concept isn't rocket science. Let's say you are on and off with someone for one year. I think it's over if you can't stay together for an entire year without breaking up five times. Also, you're probably breaking up for the same reasons each time. So really, what the fuck? If it didn't work the first time, then OK. Maybe it will work the second time around. Maybe the both of you have decided that you would like to mature and learn from your previous mistakes. Any more times that two, then you're a dependent person.

I understand why people go back to their exes. It's comfortable. You two know each other pretty well, and the both of you would rather be miserable with each other than spend a few minutes alone. But we need to be alone. If you won't take it from me, then please take it from Adam Buckley when he says "if you don't even know what you want, you're never going to find what you're looking for. Figure your own shit out first before subjecting others to it."

Serial Daters

Everyone knows at least one serial dater. The serial daters are dependent people that cannot function as a single person. I'm sure everyone has at least one Facebook friend who has a new relationship every five to six months. If you're a serial dater, you won't ever find true happiness. Serial daters need to learn to fill their emotional dependency issues on their own if they ever hope to find the right partner. I believe in quality over, well, a time filler, but I know that opinion isn't very popular in today's world.

In short, if we start loving ourselves, we can start to love others. If we keep running from ourselves, we won't ever truly love another. We can learn the basic rules of respecting other people and understand the difference between right and wrong. I thought parents taught these basic rules of society, but I guess they don't anymore.

6. WE REALLY CHEAT BECAUSE WE DON'T KNOW WHEN TO COMMIT

If you've committed to somebody for reassurance, public status, money or sex, then you committed for the wrong reason. And we know when we're committing to the wrong person, but we make excuses for our actions. I'm sure many of us have used one of the typical excuses for committing to the wrong person. I know I've made a few of these excuses too.

The "I was blinded by the sex" excuse
We're all blinded by the sex at one point or another. We know that sexual compatibility is important, but it's not the most important. You can meet someone great in the sex department, but a real piece of work outside of the bedroom. Unfortunately, we may mistake this type of person as our soulmate. They probably aren't. They just figured out the organ more so than the others we've met on our journeys. With that said, it can be difficult to distinguish between great sex and great relationships.

We may meet someone that brings us to another level sexually. But if they're nothing but a nuisance, then they need to be enjoyed during our single years. This is not a person to date. Just fuck them and enjoy it while the ride lasts, then continue on your journey. But you don't want to lose time because you were blinded by the sex. It happens to everyone at some point. The best way to avoid the trap is to notice how they act when they get lazy in the bedroom. That's when the blinders tend to come down.

I've been blinded by the sex. I really needed an aggressive guy after two years of having mediocre sex. I thought this new guy was the one. I was willing to serve him. But then he got lazy in bed. He started being very delusional. He would create something in his head then yell at me about it. He would say crude things then act like he never said them. Worst of all, he didn't let me watch the Denver Broncos kick some ass on Sundays. Needless to say, he's no longer in my life.

But I tell you this because I don't want you to be a victim to the *blinding*. It happens quickly and we need to be aware that just because a person is great in bed, doesn't mean that they're the one.

The "but I wanted to have somebody" excuse

We should never commit to a relationship because we need somebody there to hold our hand throughout life. First off, if you're dating this person for the support, you need to learn to stand on your own feet. If you continue in this relationship, you'll probably end up cheating. You may cheat because the sex is boring, the person is boring, or for revenge. You won't break up with your partner because it's nonsense to dump your support system while you get your fix. You should never commit to someone because you can't stand on your own.

You're with your current partner because it's better than being alone. But if the sex is dull, then you're going to seek it elsewhere. You probably won't tell your partner because you want that rock. You need that support system, but sadly, your support system can't give you what you need. That could be sexually or emotionally. It doesn't matter. What matters is that when you date to have someone there, then you're not comfortable with yourself. You don't love yourself, and you sure as hell won't care if you hurt someone else.

You should be single. You should NEVER date someone because you're insecure and dependent. You shouldn't commit because you're uncomfortable with making your decisions. We should learn how to do all of these things on our own. Once we take the time to know who we are and what we want, we will still date the wrong people. But! At least this time we'll be more open to learning from every relationship rather than just seeing the past partners as placeholders for our comfort and reassurance.

Moral of the story is that we need that time to ourselves in order to know who we truly want.

The "well, he/she makes me look good" excuse

For centuries, people have been dating for public admiration. We've all heard of *Pride and Prejudice*, and even if you haven't read it, you've probably heard the name. Sometimes, people think that relationships make them appear successful. Having a significant other tells the world that you're happy because you found love! Sometimes we think that having a partner makes us appear as more desirable and better than those around us. "Look, I have a boyfriend and she's been single for years. Clearly no one wants her." In fact, most of those statements aren't true. Some single people know that there's someone perfect for them and they don't care what the world thinks of their marital status.

If you're in a relationship because you think it makes you look cool or desirable, you're an idiot, and you should end that relationship before you cheat. Having a boyfriend or girlfriend doesn't make you desirable, and being with the wrong person for that reason will make you want to roam. We can't be happy with someone who isn't on the same plane as us. There can be differences, but don't establish a relationship on an unstable foundation. You'll cheat because you'll want satisfaction from elsewhere, but you don't want to lose the image you portray to the world. Save everybody some time and end the relationship. We all know it's a façade any ways.

The "I feel better about myself when I have somebody" excuse

Don't ever commit to someone because you need to be reassured that you're beautiful. First of all, beauty starts on the inside. If you have a shitty personality, you'll probably look like shit. Our physical appearances are a direct reflection of us as people. Think of the number of hot bitches that need to use lots of cosmetics to look that "hot." Don't commit to someone because you don't think you're pretty or deserving of love. Everyone is deserving of love, just not all at the same time.

It's time we realize that our self-worth doesn't rely upon how hot we're perceived by others. Our worth doesn't come from having a partner. Our self-worth starts on the inside. We must be good people that understand ourselves.

If your relationship is based on the fact that you need

reassurance about yourself, you're asking for trouble from an unstable partner.

The "but he/she has a lot of money" excuse

The gold-diggers already have a horrible reputation. Committing to someone because they have money is ridiculous. Chances are, they know that you want their money. If you find a guy and marry him for economic security, you'll be screwed when that relationship ends. This scenario typically requires a prenuptial agreement. However, a guy should know better than to marry a woman who wants his money. Now, I'm sure there are men out there who are rich and want to spoil a woman. If that's the case, then date the guy. You both know it's nothing serious, and you'll get presents. But if you choose to date someone specifically because they have money, you're making a great mistake.

It makes sense that we commit to the wrong people for the wrong reasons. We see some quality in that person that we enjoy. But sometimes we get so comfortable that we don't know when to exit the wrong relationship. We stay with the person because it's comfortable and much easier than taking another swing at the single life. But we need to know when to exit an exhausted relationship if we want to find our soulmate.

7. WE REALLY CHEAT BECAUSE WE STAY IN FAILING RELATIONSHIPS

Let's be serious, most relationships fail. The only relationship that will last is the one with your soulmate. I believe that we should only have four relationships before we meet our soulmate. I think four relationships may be pushing it, but I will give it four because it takes us a bit longer to learn from our mistakes. Now, dating and relationships are two entirely different scenarios. We go on dates because we see potential that may be shot down immediately after the first date. Dating occurs while single. Relationships occur after you meet someone that you want to see exclusively. But many of us have issues within our relationships and instead of ending a relationship due to these indifferences, we stay with our partners. The following scenarios tend to be the core issues for most relationships. If your partner mentions any of these "Red Flag" phrases, or if these "Red Flag" thoughts have crossed your mind, you may want to reconsider the relationship.

Red Flag: "Well, she wants to get married but I'm not ready"

There are plenty of women out there who want to marry young. They want a wedding and they want it in their 20s. The partner is interchangeable. I hate to say it, but there are people out there that just want to be married. Relationships founded on this basis tend to lead to an ultimatum: If you don't propose within a few years, we're done. That's just asking for a divorce. If the guy isn't sure if he wants to marry you, he shouldn't be pressured into it. If he caves in and says yes, he will propose, and most likely end up cheating in the long run. It's wrong to give a guy that ultimatum. It shouldn't matter if he proposes to you within a time frame that you have in mind.

Most couples that marry out of force tend to divorce. The guy wasn't prepared to get married but you forced it upon him. I'm all for not knowing that a guy wants to propose to me. I like surprise, but I guess I am a bit old-fashioned. But just because you want to get married and you feel like you are on a timeline doesn't mean that he is. And you sure as hell shouldn't force him into it.

Just hear yourself. If you don't propose within my time frame, we're done. Why the hell are you dating him then? Just to have a wedding? Be patient. The right person will come along and you won't need to force them to marry you.

You should never marry someone because they want to be married now. If you're not ready for a marriage, don't get married. In fact, I would dump your partner if they're pressuring you to wed when you're not ready. Don't stay in an already failed relationship.

Red Flag: "You can't watch porn because it's cheating"

Some people consider porn cheating. It's not. Get a grip. Your partner is probably just horny and you're not there to fix that problem. Most people aren't looking at porn and daydreaming about the porn star in the movie. They are watching the fucking so they can get their rocks off. Some watch it because they're into weird shit that you don't want to do. Don't be so insecure. Instead, maybe try watching porn together? Your sex life could get significantly more exciting. The point is that if you're that against your partner watching porn, then you need to fix yourself first before you commit to anyone else. Watching porn does not equate to cheating. Don't tell your partner that they can't watch porn. That's ridiculous. However, if they're a porn addict, that's just another reason to end the relationship.

Red Flag: "But I need you to survive"
I've already gone much further into the subject of dependency earlier in this book, but I will gloss over it here. Any relationship that is founded on the fact that you hate being alone is destined to fail. You should never commit to someone because you fear alone time. It's not fair to you and it sure as hell isn't fair for your partner. Most people that commit because of dependency issues have no regard for the person they're with. It's a fleeting love. You must be able to stand on your own if you plan to contribute anything to the relationship.

Red Flag: "You make me feel better about myself"
Committing to someone because you need to feel pretty and loved is even worse. You should never commit to someone because you need them there to make you feel wanted and beautiful. You need to look inside yourself and learn to love yourself first. We all hear it. You can't love anyone else until you learn to love yourself. You shouldn't commit to someone because you feel that the only way you're worthy is if you have a partner. First

off, not true. You are worthy. You just need to find that beauty within yourself. No partner can make you feel beautiful if you don't feel it yourself. In the long run, your partner will more than likely get annoyed with your insecure attitude. All of their failed attempts at telling you how beautiful you are can provoke them to leave. Then you're all alone again and on to the next person who will make you feel beautiful. It's an endless cycle.

Please try to love yourself first before forcing someone else to do it. Your relationship already failed if you're only with the person for validation.

Red Flag: "I want to be everything that you want me to be"

Don't lie, you know someone who has lost themselves in their relationship. They change their personality based on what their partner likes. They start picking up different habits and alienating their friends. They no longer are the person you once knew, but they are becoming a twin of their current partner. Often-times, our partners can pressure us into losing ourselves. It takes willpower to prevent that change. I had a partner who said that I should get tattoos and grow my hair out because it would make me more appealing to him. I said, "There's the door. Get the fuck out."

But you shouldn't lose yourself in a relationship. That person committed to you because they saw something in you that they enjoyed. Don't ruin it by trying to be them. You are what they want. Trust me, most people don't want a clone of themselves. They want someone to complement them.

If you lost yourself in a relationship, then you're not in the right relationship. We all lose ourselves at one point or another. Sometimes our goals are put on hold because we meet someone who brings us happiness. But if you ever lose touch with yourself and your inner desires, then you're in a failing relationship. The right partner doesn't try to change you or make you feel insecure about yourself. Your soulmate loves you and encourages you to be yourself.

Red Flag: "This person isn't what I desire, but is good enough for a partner"

We can find ourselves becoming impatient. We are ready to settle down and since we haven't found the one that we want to settle down with, we decide that this current one will do. Wrong decision! If you're one of the few men out there that know who you are and what you want and are willing to wait for that person, don't give up. You are in the rare 20 percent of our society and there is someone else in that 20 percent that's trying to find you.

If you find someone that will do, you're about to make a very big mistake. When it comes to establishing a family, you want to make sure that the person you choose is someone that you know you will love more and more every day. Don't just settle and say, *"you know what, I'm tired of waiting and this one is good enough. She will fit the part."* You can make this decision, but 10 years down the line, you'll regret not waiting for the right one. Your relationship may be well, but it won't bring you to the next plane, as you previously hoped.

If you've settled, you've made a colossal mistake. You'll see why when we get to the settling portion of this book.

Red Flag: "Well my partner is OK, but I am waiting for this other person to come around"

There are several people that are essentially saving someone for the future. They date other people, but in the back of their minds, they really want someone else. These people date in order to fill the time between when they meet the other person and to when they actually get to be with that person. Sadly, most people that are being saved as a back-up option probably don't want to be saved. The truth is, if you're saving someone while you're dating someone else, you're a horrible person. Not only are you wasting your time, but you're hurting and wasting your partner's time as well.

Red Flag: "But my partner is a wounded bird and I must save them"

I am almost positive that most people have been a victim to the Wounded Bird Syndrome (WBS). The WBS is when you want to fix a person. You think that they're a mess that won't be fixed until you break out your tools and start building a foundation for them. It never works. NEVER! If it does, it usually doesn't take effect until the relationship is over. At that point, you end up like Ann Perkins on Parks and Recreation: "Andy was a totally helpless baby when we met. I dated him for three years. Now he's an adult with a job. And some other girl is going to reap the rewards of my hard work? That's bullshit."

And that is exactly how it goes when you enter a relationship with the intent on fixing the wounded bird, whether for selfish or genuine reasons. I wanted to help my ex-boyfriend "The Sweet Boy". Six months after he dumped me, he got a salaried job making $100 less than me. He made 20K less than me when we dated. And now he wears suits. He looked homeless when we dated. I'm telling you, it only takes effect after the breakup.

Trying to fix a wounded bird is an exhausting process. You shouldn't date someone to fix them. They need to want to fix themselves. You can't force anyone into wanting to be fixed. However, if you're one of those people who loves saving people, I recommend that you go into counseling. You can fix the wounded birds at work, and then come home to a wonderful soulmate.

It's human nature to want to fix someone. But it's not good. It usually takes a real piece of work to divert from wounded birds. I dated a complete and total wreck. He was an infantry Marine. You could only guess how that went over. I wanted to help him. I wanted to be there for him, but he was just too much of a project and it exhausted me completely. I was always tired, sad and miserable. I kept putting his needs in front of mine and I got nowhere. Plus, it was like talking to a brick wall. Nothing ever went in those ears. After that project, I decided that I was never fixing someone ever again. I need an established man who knows who he is and what he wants. But know that you can support, comfort, understand, and provide security for a partner with a troubled past, but do so because you love them. Not to save them.

Red Flag: "Oh, but we're just fuck-buddies"

A fuck-buddy relationship rarely succeeds. More often than not, one person gets attached. The fuck-buddy relationship only works when both parties are fine with being single, but enjoy sex every now and then. Sadly, most fuck-buddy relationships are founded on some sort of emotional feeling. If one person is hoping for something more, the other should break it off. In short, a fuck-buddy relationship is difficult water to tread. Both parties need to be secure in their singleness to enjoy such a relationship.

I did have a successful fuck-buddy relationship once. It was with a co-worker from my waitressing years in college. He lived in the same apartment complex as me so the convenience was nice. He and I enjoyed drinking wine, looking for UFOs and ghosts, making money, and fucking. It started when the two of us went out for Halloween and had some fun after returning from the bar. It was awesome. It went down a few times after that, but it never affected our relationship. He wanted to be rich, I wanted to be rich. We both were very comfortable in our skin and we had no issues being single. We are great friends who sometimes fuck when we're drunk and bored. It happens. But it's a successful relationship because I don't demand a commitment from him nor him from me.

I remember the day I went over to his apartment. I got to his door as some girl was just leaving. We acknowledged each other and continued on our way. He shuts the door, looks at me, and says something like *"God, Nina. You never nagged me for a relationship after we had sex. The girl that just left had to sit me down for a conversation about where we stand because we had sex a few nights ago. Why do girls keep doing that? Sex doesn't mean relationship, but you get that."* I said something along the lines of *"of course I get it boo, because I'm in the same position as you. I don't care to have a boyfriend. That doesn't mean I don't want to get laid."*

And our friendship is still fine. We had sex because it was convenient and a hell of a lot of fun. He's a Latin boy with a rocking body and a really hot chest to upper arm tattoo. The point is that our fuck-buddy relationship worked because neither of us wanted a relationship. We wanted to get good grades, make some money, get drunk and fuck. That's it. But it's often that one of the two people gets attached, and that's why these fuck-buddy relationships tend to hit rock bottom.

If you're in a fuck-buddy relationship and one of the two of you is attached, it needs to end before someone gets hurt.

8. WE REALLY CHEAT BECAUSE WE SETTLE

Unfortunately, when we stay in failing relationships, we get comfortable. When we're comfortable, we're settling. When we settle, we cheat because we settled on someone who isn't perfect for us, but is good enough. Since most of us don't believe in fairy tales and soulmates, we accept the fact that our Prince Charming doesn't exist. There is no perfect ending, just a good enough ending.

The perfect ending does exist, but we won't have it if we keep settling.

Settling is the worst decision we could make. If we settle on someone good enough, someone is bound to cheat. Settling leads to comfort which leads to boredom. Somebody is going to cheat. There's no point in staying with someone who is good enough. Just because you're comfortable doesn't mean you're in the right relationship. Comfort makes us content. A great relationship makes us happy and complete. Think about the number of people you know who are in unsatisfactory relationships.

You may think that the person you're with now is the perfect person. If that's the case, then good for you. That doesn't happen often. However, if you have any doubts in your mind that your current partner is not all that you're looking for, then you should probably end it. There's one exception to this statement, and that's to learn what you need to learn and move on. If you continue to stay with the one person simply because it's comfortable, you'll have a worse end than if you broke it off. Now, is there a right time? I'm not sure.

I was with my ex-boyfriend for two years, and he dumped me a week before I moved to Nashville. Was it great timing? I think so. It gave me the brand new start that I really needed. I moved down to Tennessee with my cat and my career. But we both knew that we weren't meant to be together forever. It sucks when you think about it, but I did learn that not every person on this planet will leave me for an old flame. I really needed to learn that lesson. I would have been a complete wreck of a person to date had he not been so patient with me. His patience taught me that I can trust someone.

I have a feeling that kicking people out the door is difficult for any person. But, you need to be strong and do that. If the sex is boring, you're with the wrong person. If you find quirks that drive you nuts, then that person drives you nuts. There's no "getting used" to someone's quirks. There's no accepting it as it being just who they are. If who they are annoys you, then you're not with the right person. The right person thinks your quirks are cute and funny, as you them. The perfect person doesn't do things that annoy you.

The worst thing anyone can do to themselves is to stay with an incompatible partner. You love your soulmate, not tolerate them.

So how do we know if we're settling?

We're settling if we're comfortable

Comfort is the worst reason to stay with someone who doesn't elevate you to the next level. Most people go back to their exes because they know how the situation is going to end. Personally, that's the exact reason why I wouldn't waste my time going back to an ex, but I guess I'm a different brand of person. But if you feel like you can't do any better, then you won't. You might as well stay with what you already have, even if that person isn't good for your health. I don't mean to be rude, but some people are simply too lazy to go out and find someone new. So, when they need a booty call, they call up the ex. Or the thought of dating is too much of a hassle, so fuck it, might as well go back to who I know will take me.

Plus, if you stay in that comfort zone, you may end up in a slump that you can't climb out of. I strongly believe that every person hits this slump. It's the one where you're so comfortable that you stop working towards anything. You let your health go out the window, and your life becomes stagnant. This slump can last anywhere from six months to six years. Hopefully you wake up before there is no salvaging your true self.

The Slump

I hit my slump early. I was always a heavy kid. I never want to lose that much weight again, so luckily that stuck with me through the years. I hit my second slump when I was 24. I landed my dream job and a boyfriend within the same week. That's when I hit my first plateau. I was single all throughout college, so all I wanted was a great job and a wonderful boyfriend.

Well, after five years of hard work, lots of listens to Lady Gaga's "The Fame" album, and plenty of Adderall, I made my dreams come true.

After graduation, I was hired at an internet marketing company in Chicago. Within eight months, I was asked to apply for a technical writing job. I was on the fence because I felt like my skills weren't up to par, but my boss convinced me to try. I applied, interviewed, and got the job. Within a week of getting hired, I was on my first date with my now ex-boyfriend. All of my easier goals were accomplished.

I still had long-term goals, but those were put on hold because I got comfortable. I hit my first plateau and I decided to hang out for a few years. Two years to be exact. At times I wonder how different my life would've been right now had I stayed single for the past two years. But, on the bright side, he reignited my compassion and heart. Now I am warm and fuzzy Nina with a badass skill set.

But the slump drove me nuts. I hated being so stagnant. I had the motivation to continue on to my next set of goals like being a bestselling author, funding my parents' retirement, and building a shelter for Music City Animal Rescue (fostering animals does a number on the heartstrings). I had the desire, want and even the motivation. It was the "taking action" part that was so hard.

The Recovery
I knew that if I stayed in Chicago, that I would continue dating my ex-boyfriend. We would keep seeing movies, going to dinners, and drinking at the bars. I would've been doing the same things with the same people. But I needed something more, as per protocol. So I moved to Nashville in June of 2014.

Seven months after he dumped me, he told me it was because I know who I am and where I want to go in life, and he is on the opposite side of the spectrum. You may be saying, *oh Nina that is what he told you to make you feel better.* Quite possibly, but I will tell you this much; he is being honest. He's really horrible at lying. Seriously. One time I asked him if he thought I should lose weight and he said "I think you could afford to lose a couple pounds."

But I kept trying to push him because I figured it would help me push myself. I wanted him to be successful. He had such an apathetic view on life and I wanted him to be excited. I wanted him to have goals and to reach them. But I couldn't do it. He didn't share my enthusiasm. And that's why he dumped me.

And I'm OK with that because I don't want to date someone who doesn't want to keep going. I can't be with someone who chooses to have money concerns. I sure as hell can't be with a man who isn't naturally dominant. But we stayed together, mutually, for the comfort level. We had a good time, but both of us knew that it wasn't meant to last forever, but we made it last for as long as it would.

Well, that turned into a huge slump that was a horrible bitch to get out of. So my recommendation to you, my lovely readers, is that when you first start to get bored, and you know you feel comfortable, make sure to evaluate the situation. You don't want to get stuck in a place that you can't return from.

We're settling if we're trying to preserve a dead relationship

Most relationships are destined to end. Only one relationship lasts a lifetime and that's the one with your soulmate. So there's no point in trying to preserve a relationship that has already run its course. Trust me, you're just going to keep wasting your time. It doesn't matter how many years have gone into the relationship, and it doesn't matter if you had future plans. If the relationship ends, then it wasn't meant to be. Sadly, I have a friend that tried to salvage a dead relationship. It was almost the death of her.

Juliette was dating Shawn for six years. For four of those six years, he was living in Virginia while she was in Chicago. They initially broke up when Shawn moved back home, but they started dating again a few months later. During their entire relationship, neither of them was willing to move to the other's state. Finally, he decided that he may want to move back to Illinois to be with her. Juliette was beyond excited and started planning their future in one of the Chicago suburbs. She even had several apartments in mind.

He was set to fly out to Chicago so that they could look for an apartment. Unfortunately, Shawn decided to call off the flight and the relationship. He was a bit of a dick because he dumped her over the phone. He probably should have flown out and ended it in person, but what can you do? Shawn clearly didn't have much respect for her or their relationship. But Juliette wasn't willing to give up. She figured that because they already put six years into this relationship that it has to last.

Juliette spent many months trying to convince Shawn to make it work. He didn't budge. He was done with the relationship. That's fair because it happens. Just because we put time into something doesn't mean it's good. Do you know how much time and effort I put into being a great dancer? Lots, and I still suck at it. My coordination is awful, especially in a group setting. Sure, I can do some twirls and leg spins, but I'm not dancing for Britney Spears anytime soon. Being a dancer isn't my destiny and I accept that.

Sometimes the person we're with isn't our soulmate, and we need to accept what we learned and move on.

We're settling when we tolerate our partner

You're not supposed to tolerate friends or lovers. We tolerate co-workers, people at the supermarket and customers at our jobs, but we don't tolerate the people we choose to be around. If your partner annoys you, then break up. Don't stay with them because soon you'll grow to hate that person.

We're a society that has an issue with settling on a commitment and hoping for the best. But we wouldn't settle if we knew who we were. If we can understand our desires and act on them during our single years, we'll have legendary relationships with our soulmates. But introspection is much needed. So when we find ourselves in unsatisfactory relationships, we must know when to exit.

Know When to Exit

The worst thing we could do is try to preserve a relationship because we've invested too much time into it. If the relationship isn't working, then the relationship doesn't work. We shouldn't put our lives on hold because we planned to marry this person. Just because your relationship lasted for so many years doesn't mean it's meant to last a lifetime.

There are always lessons to be learned. We just need to acknowledge the signs and explore new routes. Life doesn't always go according to plan. You should be thankful for the detour. Life just saved you from a huge mistake. If something inside is telling you to end it, you should listen to that inner voice.

The Downside of Staying Friends

So you've left the relationship. What now? Do we stay friends? No. It's one thing to remain friendly, and it's another thing to remain friends. For instance, if I saw my ex-boyfriend "The Sweet Boy" at a restaurant, we would be friendly, but I wouldn't ask "The Sweet Boy" to watch a movie with me. And if you're in a new relationship, it's time to cut ties with your ex. Your current partner is there to provide you with that love and care, not your ex.

But, most of us stay friends with our exes. Sometimes it makes sense when no one was terribly hurt in the breakup, but I'm sure that's an unusual scenario. Most of the time, one of the two people is hurt. Don't remain friends if one of you is seriously hurt. If you're the one hurting, you should eliminate that person from your life. If you're the dumper, stop talking to the person you hurt. You're leading them on and giving them false hope. It's not healthy for your ex and it's not good for your new relationship. Sadly, my friend Lana is currently a heartbroken victim to a disrespectful ex-boyfriend. Let me tell you a little bit about her.

Lana is wonderful. She is nice, pretty, smart, and has a lucrative career, but she has been a mess as of late. She dated this boy for two years, and at one point they were sharing an apartment. He ended their relationship about two years ago, but she hasn't given up hope. He says that they can stay friends, so they hang out even though he knows that she still has feelings for him. Lana believes that she will still get her ex, even if he has a new girlfriend. She is putting her life on hold for this boy. She has spent many nights crying and downing bottles of wine. She has found herself in a relentless cycle.

What's worse is that her ex-boyfriend sees the effect that his actions have on her. I would love to smack her across the face and say *"GET OVER IT! He's not the one for you. You need to cut him off completely."* But as we know, these conversations never end well. So this is why I'm addressing the dumpers; if you dumped your partner and they still love you, cut them loose. Sometimes the ones that are hurting will never give up hope if you keep providing it. You're damaging your old flame and you're ruining your current relationship if you keep your ex on the hook.

And this is just her story. I know for a fact that this situation happens far more often than we would like to admit. It's fair to want to stay friends with your ex. You two had great times together and you don't want to lose the friendship. But that friendship is on the line the instant you start dating. It doesn't matter if you were friends beforehand. Relationships break friendships.

It is possible to stay friendly with an ex, just not likely. The only time where exes are friendly is when the relationship didn't end horribly. Sometimes people realize that they're not with the right person and sometimes that feeling is mutual. They both decide that it was a good run, but it wasn't meant to last forever. They accept that and move on. One may take it worse than the other, but the underlying reason was agreed upon.

The point is this: Don't stay friends with your ex. Nothing good comes out of that friendship.

PART 3: EFFECT ON SOCIETY

Cheating has not only dismantled our view of love, but it's having a detrimental effect on our society. We believe that the idea of true love is so farfetched that our way of adapting has been to commit to the wrong people, and then cheat on them.

Our cheating behavior and the justification for it is pushing society to a breaking point. We're becoming sensitive, dependent, entitled and justified all at the same time! On top of that, we have little to no respect for relationships. We're not a society of enlightened people listening to their intuitions. Instead, we're a group of people that feel so dependent on relationships that we don't know ourselves or the problems we cause for those around us. Quite frankly, we don't care either. The children are the ones suffering from our nonsensical relationship choices, but we're not suffering, so it doesn't matter. We need to take a step back to see what has happened to us as a society.

9. WE'RE TOO SENSITIVE

We're a sensitive culture. I know that statement is going to piss a lot of people off, but I'm taking a risk here. So please, I'm begging you to not get offended but try to listen to what I'm saying. I never thought I would do this, but I'm going to quote Adam Levine and how he won over a contestant on The Voice. "My honest opinion is that there are definitely some things I heard that need a little bit of work. My goal is to make you better. That's how I work with my team. I'm going to put myself on the line by saying that because not everyone likes to hear that. But it's the people that like to hear it that go the distance."

We can have wonderful and fulfilling lives if we're willing to understand our insecurities instead of denying them. But we hate ourselves. We hate ourselves so much that if we possess any trait that's deemed a "bad quality", we get defensive, say we're not like that and move on. Instead of trying to understand why we act the way we do, we say the other person is an asshole and we continue to act the same. Now there is a difference between being told that you're dependent and being told you should get a nose job. If someone says you need a nose job, that person is just a dick.

The point is that we all have flaws. We should all understand that no one is perfect, yet if one of our imperfections is mentioned, we go ape shit. It happens. We all do it. We are humans and we don't like being told anything that rivals our own beliefs. But my thought is, that you won't be offended if it doesn't apply to you. We can find laws proving that statement wrong, I'm sure, but I think it's the case for most situations. For instance, let's say that your friend said that you're a horrible driver. Are you offended? Probably, because it's your driving that they're insulting. Let's say that the same person said your other friend is a horrible driver. Would you be offended by that statement now?

What super blows my mind is how we get offended by stuff that we can easily avoid. You can't tell me that Daniel Tosh offends you so he should lose his job. There is this thing called a remote and it changes channels. You don't need to watch Daniel Tosh if he offends you. I won't watch that show during dinner because he's always showing something gross. I solve this issue by migrating over to TruTV.

Truth be told we prefer being right over being logical. If you don't believe me, look at Congress. Both parties just want to be right, no one wants to find a solution. We don't want to find a solution because we don't like hearing things we oppose. We never learn because it's easier to be offended and disregard sensible cooperation.

10. WE'RE TOO DEPENDENT ON RELATIONSHIPS

We're so sensitive that if someone says we're dependent, we immediately defend our positions. But we are a dependent group of people, and we always have a partner because we need someone there. Being dependent on relationships only leads to unhappiness. Instead of accepting as fact that people are naturally dependent, it's time to take responsibility for ourselves. Relationships are screwy because instead of entering relationships for valid reasons, we jump in for validation. But instead of trying to improve ourselves so that we can improve the lives of others, we decide it's better to live a standard life with a mediocre partner.

We have more than enough dependent people in our society. Dependent people are the ones who struggle to be alone at night. They're the ones relying on a partner to make them feel OK about themselves. Some people are even incapable of functioning without a partner. Dependent people believe that as long as they have a partner, their life is perfect. I hate to be so blunt, but we all know that these people exist. Luckily for the dependents, there is a cure. Some call it self-esteem.

Now I do understand that there are certain events that can happen in one's past causing them to be dependent. A woman raised without a father may be more dependent on a partner. They need someone to fill the void that their father was supposed to fill. The same thing can happen to men, too. I'm sure that if a man loses his mother in one form or another, that loss can cause them to be dependent on a partner.

But, once again, there is a cure for this mishap. We have the choice of being defined by our past or learning from it. We can become the people that we're meant to be if we attempt to learn from life struggles, or we can stay stagnant and live a life of mediocrity, always seeking pity and comfort. We all want to know the point of our existence, but we will never know anything if we refuse to learn from our mistakes.

So, if you find yourself as one of these dependent people, you may want to start being comfortable in your skin. Not only is dependency detrimental to one's happiness, but it can have an effect on your partner as well. Think about a couple where one is overly dependent. The dependent one doesn't want their partner to do anything without them. Well, the more independent partner is more than likely to get annoyed. Whether or not they have the courage to break it off or not is another story, but it usually ends with cheating or dumping.

The worst part about dependency is that dependent people don't care who the partner is, as long as they have someone there. I'm sure you've seen the girls who *must* be married young. As long as they're married by 25, the spouse is irrelevant. Also, not a good plan. When you give your partner an ultimatum in regards to marriage, you're essentially asking for a divorce. The guy wasn't prepared, but he was stupid and caved in anyways. I give these marriages three years of bliss, tops, or maybe on year of bliss and two years of hell.

Lucky for you dependent people, it's not all your fault.

Social Media Promotes Dependency

You can place some of the blame on our society. Our society not only supports dependency, but promotes it as well. Look at Taylor Swift. She has multiple songs about how a guy belongs to her, how that guy breaks her heart, and then how she is on to the next. The worst part is that millions love her. There are also many dependent people making decisions about how the public should view relationships and that's a dangerous game.

One perfect example of wrong people providing horrible advice is found in a Buzzfeed video called *The Terrifying Truth about Being Single.*[4] If you haven't seen it yet, you should probably watch it. But I cannot paste a Buzzfeed video into a hardcover book, so I will give you the synopsis of this video, and you can look it up in the references if you're interested in seeing the video. The ridiculousness does make it worth a watch.

This video opens with Kyle telling his friends that he wants to be single because he's bored in his relationship. Clearly, he's already reconsidering the relationship, that is, until his two friends burst through the door with poor advice.

His first friend wants him to stay with Jenna so that he can avoid living alone. Apparently, his friend didn't know how to live alone, and instead jerked off for an entire month straight and forgot how to do his laundry.

His second friend wants him to stay with Jenna so that he can continue showering. I guess this second friend forgot how to turn on the shower without a girlfriend around. Then both friends continue to lecture him on the horrors of being single. These horrors include not watching feminine movies, or having nice things, or eating good food.

Regardless of their efforts, Kyle continues to plea his case by stating that if he were single, then he could go out to trivia night with his friends. But the only reason his friends even go to trivia night is to find a girlfriend, and he already has a girlfriend. Then they decide to scare the shit out of him by suggesting that the only girls available are psychopaths who are obsessed with Instagramming every moment of the new relationship.

And you know what? That does the trick. Kyle is now terrified of being single because there is nothing left out there. So, in the end, Kyle stays with his girlfriend to live miserably ever after.

So there you have it. The terrifying truth about being single is that you will be on your own, left to your own devices, in a world full of psychopaths. What I'm wondering is how in the hell is this sane behavior?

If Kyle is bored, then he isn't with the right woman, especially if that woman doesn't allow him to enjoy his friends. Kyle shouldn't stay with Jenna because he can't do laundry or manage his masturbation time. He should break up with Jenna to find not only himself, but a partner who truly understands his needs.

Music Promotes Dependency
There is no need to be ashamed of being a dependent person. Our culture promotes dependency, probably because love makes money. Think of the amount of

money that Valentine's Day takes in. Then you have expensive resorts, fancy restaurants, and weekend trips all dedicated to a couple's outing. But besides all of those money makers, where do you think love makes the most amount of money? You probably guessed right; the music industry.

Let's just take a glance at Taylor Swift. She's the perfect example of marketing love to the masses. You can probably only name two songs that aren't about a lover.

Quite honestly, I don't think Taylor Swift is the best role model for young women. She continues to make the same mistakes. Even when she knows she's making a mistake, she still goes for it. Her songs preach dependency. She is constantly searching for this love, but she doesn't even know who she is yet. Personally, I would love to be her life coach. If I had the chance to show her how to spend her money, she would have a much better time.

But I must admit, the song that kills me is *I Knew You Were Trouble.* If you knew the guy was trouble, why did you then proceed to date the guy, inevitably get your heart broken and then make the rest of us sane people suffer through your nonsense? I don't think we should promote the idea of walking into a bad situation. Now I get that we need to make the mistakes in order to learn from them, but it's pretty clear that poor Tay Tay has learned this lesson on multiple occasions. And Taylor Swift is not the only culprit here. Personally, I think that Adele is worse. I just had to mention her because she is the Pop Queen of the heartbreak songs.

After all, there was the emo phase. I hope that emo music has fallen off the radar of the younger generation. Talk about instilling dependency within your audience. Talk about making the idea of love much worse. In short *"if you don't love me during my teenage angst years, I am going to cut myself and commit suicide."* Yeah, not a great message to send to unstable, dependent teenagers.

So like I said, don't necessarily blame yourself for having dependency issues. After all, Taylor Swift and emo music don't help the situation.

Now although I say don't completely blame yourself, that doesn't mean you should accept it. Don't let Taylor Swift justify your dependency issues. Learn to love yourself. Then go find someone else who is also OK with themselves and is a match for you.

11. WE'RE INCAPABLE OF TAKING RESPONSIBILITY

We have no idea how to take responsibility for our actions. If we're confronted with something, we automatically make excuses for our actions. We do this at work, at home, and in our personal relationships. We always place the blame on someone or something else. If we make a mistake at work, we blame it on the surrounding circumstances instead of the fact that we may have forgotten to do something. If a friend asks you to be nicer, we yell excuses as to why we're treating them poorly.

The number of people that refuse to take responsibility for their actions is mind blowing. I wonder how we ever expect to move forward as a society if we can't admit when we're wrong. And most of the time it isn't even about someone being wrong, it's about someone hurting someone else. And, instead of caring that we hurt someone, we make excuses for why we act the way we did. We live in a time where everything that happens is someone else's fault. It's never our fault.

I had quite a few friends in college who refused to take responsibility for their actions. One was my old friend Kim. I always helped her out because I enjoyed her. She was nice, fun, and beautiful. We both had troubled childhood years. Her parents were divorced and had some money troubles, so I always helped her out any way I could. I even got her hired as a server at the restaurant where I worked.

One day, her father had a stroke. He survived and is functioning normally now, but I do understand the severity of the situation. So when that happened, we told her that we would cover her shifts for the rest of the week. Three weeks later, we scheduled her back on for spring break. We told her that she was to work on Wednesday. She decided not to show up. But then I texted her and asked her why she didn't come in. She said that she didn't need to because of what her father went through. I asked her if someone told her that she was on the schedule and she said "Yes." I asked why she didn't call in and she told me that it was none of my damn business. She said I'm a horrible person and that I could never understand what it felt like to have a parent in the hospital. Well, my mother had a heart attack when I was 12, breast cancer when I was 21, and uterine cancer when I was 22. I think I know what it's like to have a parent in the hospital.

But instead of just saying "*I am sorry I should have called in*" she relentlessly attacked me.

But this isn't uncommon in our society. It happens all the time in the career world too. Lots of people hate being told that they need improvement. Well, if someone has been doing your job for 20 years longer than you have, they probably have sound advice.

12. WE HAVE NO RESPECT FOR RELATIONSHIPS

We have no respect. We only care about ourselves and what we want. And it's not just in relationships. We don't respect people, period. Some people have no respect for their roommates; some people have no respect for other people's relationships. Either way, we don't have respect for people the way that we should.

The Disrespectful Roommate

I had a roommate in college who had no respect for anyone. She didn't go to school or pay for her rent. She just existed in our apartment while I was working two serving jobs and attending school fulltime. She was very dependent. She always had a boyfriend and could not exist without someone telling her that she's beautiful. The scary part is that she was gorgeous, on the outside. But it brings me back to a time when I asked her if she would keep her public displays of affection (PDA) with the boyfriend to her room. It came down to the fact that I had to eat dinner in my room if I didn't want to watch her and her boyfriend making out. Finally, I got annoyed with it and politely asked if she could keep the PDA in her bedroom. She plugged both of her ears with her index fingers and said "NA, NA, NA, I don't want to hear it!"

I was pissed off. A week later, I walked into the kitchen to get some orange juice and she was getting ass-rammed on the kitchen counter. She said that she didn't know I was home. I was pissed because she didn't care that her constant PDA upset me. I asked her a week before if she could compromise and simply keep the sex in her bedroom. She had no concern for my feelings.

She only cared about herself. In the end, she blamed me because I was the inconsiderate asshole. Well, I was studying two majors, working as the newsletter editor for STC-NIU and waitressing at two restaurants. She was smoking weed and having sex all day.

Basically, we need people to realize that hurting other people isn't a good thing.

The Disrespectful Ass
We also have no respect for relationships. With multiple blogging sites promoting cheating, you also come across sites that teach you how to steal a woman from her boyfriend. How rude are these people that they would actually consider stealing a partner from another person? If someone is successful in stealing a person from someone else, the stealer must consider that the person who was stolen will probably be stolen again; and that person isn't a winner if you can easily sway them out of their current relationship.

If someone leaves their current relationship for reasons other than the relationship wasn't working, then stay away. And what kind of asshole tries to snag another man's girlfriend? There are plenty of women out there and one is right for you. Don't be a douche. I mean, I get that most of us don't know what we want, but who are you to say that you know what that other person needs? Come on, son.

And the complete disregard for the other person's relationship leads me to believe that relationships today mean nothing. Relationships are here to fulfill our desires. We don't care about our partners at all. We have de-evolved. We haven't grown to understand the beauty of companionship. Instead, we see companionship as a necessity for survival. It's almost like food and water.

But relationships should mean something.

13. WE MAKE BAD DECISIONS

We need to start taking ourselves and others seriously. Cheating has defeated us. People now enter relationships with the expectation of either cheating or being betrayed by a cheater. Our trust for one another is diminishing. Our views on marriage are so skewed that people sign prenuptial agreements preparing for a divorce. Why? Because we're so dependent on relationships that we marry the wrong people. And the fucked up part is that most of us know that we're marrying the wrong person. But, we still do it anyway.

We're marrying for the wrong reasons

We tend to marry the wrong people for our selfish reasons. We want to be married young. We're afraid that if we're not married, then we'll be alone forever. We need someone there to help us survive because it's much easier when we have a partner than it is when we're alone. What's worse is that our society has justified this poor behavior rather than attempting to understand the problems and fixing it them. We're too impatient.

Marriage cannot be a rushed decision. According to Psychology Professor Scott Stanley at the University of Denver, most marriages today either end in divorce or marital stress. He makes the following points based on his research regarding couple development, marital distress and divorce prevention.[5]

- About 31 percent of a person's friends, aged 35 to 54, who are married, engaged or cohabiting have already previously been married.

- People who have been married many years (say, 35-plus) and have never been divorced have almost no chance of the marriage ending in divorce.

- The rate of divorce per year per 1,000 people has been declining since 1980.

- A young couple marrying for the first time today has a lifetime divorce risk of 40 percent, "unless current trends change significantly."

Although the above points may seem of concern to a small group of individuals, it should concern anyone who cares about finding their soulmate. We cannot let our desire for love rush us to the altar. You'll miss out on your soulmate if you marry for the wrong reasons.

Choosing who to marry is something that takes thorough consideration. Don't give up on waiting for that right person. That right person is on their way and they're taking the express train. If you're in the common group of people and like it there, then marry for your invalid reasons; but don't be surprised when it ends in divorce.

If you're a well-rounded man that's looking for your soulmate, but you're growing impatient, please wait a little longer. Never marry someone because they fulfill the position just enough. Your wife is someone who you'll adore for the rest of your life. That wife will be the mother of your children. You can't give that title to anyone who is simply "close enough." You'll be unhappy. We need to listen to our inner selves. Our inner selves will bring us to our soulmate if we just listen. Your perfect person is out there, and they're trying to find you just as much as you're trying to find them. I promise. And don't marry someone with who you'll need to sign a prenuptial agreement.

We're all for Prenuptial Agreements

Divorce is so common that people rarely marry without a prenuptial agreement. We expect our marriage to fail. That is how deranged our ideals of love are. We no longer believe that true love exists. We no longer believe that an everlasting marriage is a possibility. Instead, we expect our marriages to fail, from boredom or cheating.

Personally, I wouldn't sign a prenuptial agreement because that makes me assume that the guy is expecting our relationship to end. He already has an "out" of the marriage. That's messed up. I get that it's safe for money reasons, but if you think your fortune will be in danger due to the marriage, you shouldn't get married. I plan on marrying someone that I know I will be with forever. Not someone who I'll be unsure about within a few years.

I understand that, in case of a divorce, you don't want to lose your assets. But going into a marriage with the idea that it will end in a divorce is absolute nonsense. You shouldn't marry someone that you don't trust. You shouldn't marry someone that you think will bore you in years to come. You shouldn't marry someone for the sake of marrying. You shouldn't marry someone because you think that they're good enough for the purpose of marriage and family, but they aren't what you truly want. If you're marrying someone for the right reasons, you won't have that inability to trust them. You wouldn't think that they're going to run away with all of your money.

If a man proposed to me and then asked me to sign a prenuptial agreement, I will show him the door. I may have killed my odds with most men out there for saying that, but it's the truth. Personally, I don't commit to people that I don't see a future with, but many in society do. I mean, really? You're going to consider marrying someone that you already think you may divorce later on? It's not being prepared; it's being pessimistic and unsure.

True love exists. If we stop being stupid, learn to love ourselves, and learn to be patient, we will have happier marriages. We will no longer enter a life commitment with the idea of divorce lingering in the background. We won't marry someone that has the right qualities for a spouse, but not the qualities that you desire in a spouse. You don't want just any man to be the father of your children, and you don't want just any woman to be the mother of your children.

We're not setting good examples for the children

The need for love and care starts at an early age, and if we can change the way adults view love now, then maybe we can create a better future for our children.

We all know that the children are the future of our society. Do we really want to raise a bunch of entitled boys and girls that can't function on their own? No. We need to step back and think about who we want to help raise our family. If we're feeling OK about the person, but not great, then you're just going to put all of your troubles onto your children. Loveless marriages lead to irresponsible parenting. We might as well just start having arranged marriages because if we keep going down this path, we're going to run out of options.

If we keep making poor relationship decisions, our children are going to have no example of what true love is. We're going to have a significant increase in single parents and depressed children. Children need to follow a good example. That includes instilling morals, raising them right, and showing them what true love is. But you can't show a child what true love is if you don't know what it means.

And if you don't believe that divorce truly impacts the children, then these statistics just might do the trick. According to DivorceSource.com,[6] children raised in fatherless homes are more likely to make poor decisions. Their data states that "children from fatherless homes account for 63 percent of youth suicides, 71 percent of the pregnant teenagers, 90 percent of the homeless and runaway children, and 70 percent of the institutionalized juveniles. They account for 85 percent of the children with behavioral disorders, 80 percent of rapists, 71 percent of all high school dropouts, 75 percent of all adolescent patients in chemical abuse centers and 85 percent of all youths in prison."

It's essential for children to grow up in a loving household. But they can't do that if we keep making stupid relationship mistakes. We can't keep marrying to have a spouse. We need to marry out of want. We need to choose our partners wisely. We must settle down with the right person, not settle on a person who "does the trick".

Children need love from their parents. But how can a child feel loved if their parents are divorced? More often than not, children believe that they're the cause for a divorce. Although that statement may not always ring true, the fact is that the child is carrying the burden of their parents who married for the wrong reasons. Essentially, dependency on relationships is causing our children grief, and that's unacceptable. We need to learn how to be independent. It may be easier to cope with life by having a partner, but life isn't meant to be easy, and we must learn how to stand on our own.

The more people begin to marry the ones that are perfect for them, the better the life for the children. We have one too many children being thrown in orphanages because parents are incapable of caring for them. The amount of teens that come from divorced parents is outlandish. It's more of a rarity to find a young adult with married parents. It just doesn't happen anymore.

We need to stop committing to the wrong people for the wrong reasons. We need to listen to our intuition. Do you want to experience that love at first sight feeling? You can, you just need to know who you are first or else you won't recognize your counterpart's soul. We can't keep settling then cheating. It's a dangerous cycle that affects everybody.

If we ever hope to solve this cheating issue, we must first learn how to embrace our single years.

PART 4: BE SINGLE

It's a terrifying concept, but there's nothing wrong with being single. After all, you can't stand on your own if you don't know how to be alone. If you're single, you'll learn far more about yourself and what you want in life. You can explore your sexual desires while finding your path. You can learn the most when you listen to your higher self. But you can't hear your inner voice if you need to fill that void with the voice of another.

We're so desperate that we settle with whoever offers to tolerate us. We're so scared of being alone. We're so afraid of understanding ourselves. We're so frightened of silence that we cannot stand to be alone with our own thoughts. We must be distracted because time with ourselves is the most terrifying concept. Why is this?

Personally, I love being alone and doing things that no one else will judge me for because they don't know what I'm doing. But most of us would rather tolerate the presence of another human being than to be alone. That's how low we've sunk.

But because we would rather have someone there than no one at all, we marry the wrong person. We begin to think that maybe if we just took that time to be alone. Took the time to figure out who we really are and what we want out of life. But, it is far too late for that. The last 10 years of our lives included tolerating another human being and trying to raise a child with that person. We struggled, fought, and now we have to divide our belongings and time with our children.

It's an avoidable mistake.

14. THE BENEFITS OF BEING SINGLE

You should be able to be happy on your own. Dealing with challenges on your own teaches you how to think logically, how to be strong and how to solve future problems. You should love who you are and your body, and realize that any person who gets to date you is a lucky person. Don't get too cocky. Humble is always the high road. Cherish yourself. If you don't love yourself, can't make yourself happy, and can't handle challenges on your own, then you're not ready to help elevate another person.

We need to recognize and remember the wonders of being single.

Masturbation

I know it may be a bit taboo, but masturbation is pretty great. A main reason I would choose sex over masturbation is to feel the touch of another human. And sometimes we all just need to get laid. It happens. Unfortunately, a lot of people are afraid of masturbating. Odd if you ask me. How would you know if sex is good if you haven't tested your own equipment? We all like different things, and you won't know what you like if you haven't experimented.

But think of all of the other benefits of masturbating.

- You get to fuck who you want to fuck, mentally. Want to fuck Chris Hemsworth? Done.
- No pregnancy
- No STDs
- You get it done right
- You can fall asleep afterwards and not have to worry about pleasing the other person

There's nothing wrong with masturbating. Personally, I'm a fan of all the benefits. I don't have time for a kid or a sexually transmitted disease. I like that I get what I want and can fall asleep afterwards. Sure, there isn't someone there making you feel pretty, but honestly, looks have no impact on getting laid. People love sex and they will fuck anything. Sex doesn't make you beautiful. True beauty comes from within.

Sexual Experience
We saw earlier that someone suggested cheating on your partner so that you can gain the sexual experience. No. You do that while single. While you're single, you can have sex with anyone you want to. Being single is the PERFECT TIME to get experience. I don't know what kinds of drugs society is on, but I prefer for my future husband to have had his practice during his single years.

Personally, I don't think one-night stands are horrible. It makes less sense for me to think about people pairing off with a person that they fucked one night while drunk. Then again, I live life more Lady Gaga the Fame style. Sometimes I've slept with people just to see if I could. I also went on dates for free dinners and practice. We all have done it.

You can get the most amount of sexual experience while you're single. There's no reason to commit to one person after you have a drunken sexcapade.

Freedom
Good God, the freedom! When you're single, you get to do what you want. You have no one holding you

back, no one to disapprove of your actions. There is no one to be against your way of life. Life is about making mistakes and learning from them. How will you ever know who you are or what you want if you can't stand to be alone with yourself? How would you know if you're with the right person if you haven't taken the time to be yourself?

Have a bucket list? You don't need a partner to knock some goals off the list. You want to go to Amsterdam? Grab a couple friends and go to Amsterdam. Or go alone. It doesn't matter. The point is to have experiences without someone depending on you. You need to see the world. You need to step away from your doorstep in order to know anything about yourself.

I do understand comfort, but comfort is a ball and chain and the opposite of freedom. If you're afraid to leave your hometown, you may be stuck in a circle of death. And it's not the fun kind of Circle of Death where you get hammered. Comfort disables freedom. Comfort is where you decide that you are fine with what you have and you no longer need to seek anything else out of life. Well, 10 years from now, you'll regret that decision. That's where regrets come from. Not doing everything that we wanted to do when we had the chance. Well, being single is our time to travel the world, explore ourselves, and do the things that we want to do. Plus, having these experiences on our own teaches us far more about life rather than when we have a partner with us.

Let's say you go to Amsterdam with your partner. Unless your partner is cool, which rarely happens, then you're stuck spending all of the time with your partner. Say goodbye to meeting people from that country. Say goodbye to hanging out with a group of Brazilians that you meet while on your travels. Say goodbye to making the decision to do anything because you have to consider what the other person wants you two to do.

That's not a great experience in a foreign country.

Personal Time
I know that most people loathe personal time. It's a shame, really. Personal time is when we get to know ourselves. Personal time helps us break free from the stress of the modern world and retreat to our own fantasy land. The truth is we all need time to figure ourselves out. I know that I've said that on multiple occasions, but no one seems to want to take the time to know themselves. I wouldn't stress it so often if it weren't an issue. We need to look into ourselves. Find out who we are and where we want to go. We need to at least attempt to love and understand ourselves before we commit to anyone else. We need to have a platform for the relationship.

That personal time helps us greatly. And there is no shame in getting laid while trying to find our personal path. See, we get to grow and fuck while we're single.

Personal Growth
We always hear that men mature so much later than women. In my experience, they tend to mature at the same age. I've seen plenty of immature girls in their late 20s. We struggle to mature and grow because we're so distracted. We're distracted by the news, music and

most importantly, Facebook. Facebook really fucked up a generation. Myspace wasn't that serious. In this day and age, kids seek validation from their peers on Facebook. They're too busy trying to outdo one another that no one pays attention to their own life and their own path.

As unfortunate as it sounds, we need to recognize the error in our ways if we ever plan to grow up. Part of growing up is making mistakes, understanding, and then learning from those mistakes. Part of growing up is acknowledging our behavior and its effect on others around us. Growing up is being able to stand on our own. Grow up so that you don't need anyone else to survive.

We live in an entitled society. Too many youths no longer pay for their own rent until their mid-20s. They always have someone to fall back on if their lives turn out differently than they hoped. But these people don't grow up. These people remain the same until something drastic happens that makes them want to change their lives. Being single is a great time to learn how to finance ourselves. We learn from our mistakes, we learn how to balance a check book, and we learn more about what we want to be when we leave college.

You can't know any of that if you don't take college seriously. College is the foundation for the rest of your life. Granted, not everyone can go to college. But for those of you that do and for those that plan to, I highly recommend going away to college and taking that experience seriously.

15. THE COLLEGE YEARS (OR THE BEST TIME TO BE SINGLE)

The cost of education is ridiculous. Trust me; I went to an iffy school that has been insulted by ESPN on multiple occasions. And I'm still paying off my student loans. I get that the education system in our country is completely fucked. But! That doesn't mean that going away to college doesn't have its merits.

I wish I could make everyone go away to school, rather than going to community college, or a college in a big city. I want people to experience the college town life. Living in a town where there is just you and 20,000 other people your age and about 15,000 townies, you learn more about your life than anywhere else. Not only does everyone in a college town have the same agenda (going to school, working, and partying), but they're all experiencing life and learning from each other. Well, at least those that understand the true purpose of college do these things.

It's just like one of my English professor's told me, "If you have gone to college and you haven't had your core shaken, then you didn't experience college."

I've seen more than enough people pairing off in college. I believe that if most people stayed single throughout college, they could get the sexual experience, as well as the learning experience they need for their foundation. Being single during the time when you're meant to learn the most really teaches you. College is the time when you're supposed to find yourself and your path. The general education courses help you define the career path you want to take. Living in a dormitory with 50 other students on your floor teaches you how to get along with people from various backgrounds. Having ultimate freedom with the expectation of going to classes teaches you responsibility. Paying for your own apartment in college teaches you how to budget your money.

College also offers plenty of opportunities for you to obtain a career in the field you want. You just need to acknowledge the signs. There are open doors everywhere from student organizations to internships. Being single in college helps you see all of these openings. You're not distracted with the fact that your partner may be your soulmate. You're concentrated on who you really are and where you're going. I recommend that everyone that goes away to school to try and stay single throughout the experience. Getting laid in college is very easy. You might as well get all of your sexual fantasies out during college. That's the time and place where everyone else is trying to fulfill their fantasies. Try some drugs, do all that you can't do in the career field. Understand that college is the only time and place where you can have that complete and total freedom.

That said, college students fall into one of the following categories.

- Sleep, Social Life, Bad Grades
- Good Grades, Sleep, No Social Life
- Good Grades, Social Life, No Sleep

I recommend the third point. You'll have plenty of time to sleep after you graduate. You might as well get good grades and party. That's the whole point of college. It teaches you some excellent time management skills.

Being single throughout college teaches you to be independent. After all, dependency is a huge reason as to why relationships fail.

But if you're an adult, the dating game is horrible. I know this, but that doesn't mean that we should give up! There's someone out there for us. We shouldn't consume our years trying to find that person. We should live our lives and let fate bring us to our soulmate. We struggle to find our soulmates because we're so impatient. We want someone to fill that position now. Well, there are plenty of things to do on this planet. Do the things that you want to do and watch how life brings you to your prize at the end of the game.

We're adults. We're well-rounded individuals, and our soulmates will find us.

16. BECOME IN TUNE WITH YOUR INTUITION

Being single teaches us not to settle. Discovering ourselves creates a genuine belief that we will get what we deserve. But we can't find our soulmate if we don't listen to ourselves. You know that little voice in your head? That is your higher self or your intuition. Our intuition leads us down the right path. Ever hear a thought in your head that sounded like a good idea? Go through with it. The same goes for bad ideas. If you have a bad feeling about something, it's best to not do that something.

Our intuition is what brings us to our soulmate. It's what guides us through this life so that we can find our other half. We all come into this world with an other half, but we can't find them if we don't listen to our higher self. Our higher selves have the road map that leads directly to the light at the end of the tunnel: our soulmate. But we can't reach our destination if we don't listen to the cartographer.

Ever since we're children, our intuition notifies us when it finds something that we look for in our soulmate. Think to when you first discovered your sexual orientation. What was it that triggered the thought that you sexually like something? And this does happen when we're children and often because that's when we're most likely to listen. For instance, I remember when my intuition triggered me about my sexual preference. I was 12 years old, I heard a Boston accent, and immediately I knew that men won the battle over my sexual orientation.

Our soulmate checklist is entirely compiled by things that our intuition has triggered inside of us, and we listened. We all have different paths. We like different things, but there is one person out there that loves you for all that you are and you love them for the same reason. This true love happens because you've heard your inner voice. You heard it crying out to you and you listened. It's only when we start listening to ourselves and doing what we want that we meet our soulmates.

Let your inner voice guide you to your soulmate.

PART 5: SOULMATES

Our soulmate is out there, it's just a matter of enjoying our journey as life leads us to that person. We shouldn't commit to someone who we think isn't right for us. We should wait and enjoy our years the best that we can, and our soulmate will be waiting on the other side of our climb.

When you commit to someone that means that you want to be there for them, through the good and the bad. You commit to them because you don't want anyone else to have them. You adore this person and you want to be the one that they spend the rest of their life with. You commit to someone because you feel a deep attraction to them. You commit because that person is attractive inside and out. You commit because you enjoy them. You wouldn't want to commit to someone that is just there to fulfill one specific need. You commit because they fulfill all of your needs.

But we believe that true love is so unattainable that we accept dependence and justification as a way of life. At the rate we're going, true love will eventually cease to exist. Thanks to a bunch of assholes trying to prove cheating as a way to save dead-end relationships, the good people that believe in true love will become extinct from society. But love is such a powerful force that is being taken for granted. It breaks my heart.

Love is the most powerful force on the planet. I know that we hear it and dismiss it as nonsense, but that's only because we don't acknowledge it. Have you ever had a moment where you felt sick just to find out that a family member had something horrible happen to them? We disregard it, but the power of love transcends all planes, and I've felt it.

My brother was hit while riding his motorcycle on the morning of my 26th birthday. I was in Tennessee and he was in Chicago. A few of my best friends came down to Nashville to celebrate, so we went downtown. But I'm a grandma and was in bed by 1 a.m. At 3:30 a.m., I woke up crying over my ex-boyfriend, "The Sweet Boy". It was strange because I was passed out drunk, out like a light. Then, all of a sudden, I was awake and crying out "The Sweet Boy's" name. I didn't understand why I was in such hysterics over the breakup because I never cried like that over him.

I eventually fell back asleep and woke up around 11 a.m. My mother called me to say "Happy Birthday" followed by, "I'm at the hospital. Paul was taken to the emergency room." My brother Paul was hit on his motorcycle. The lady driving her SUV didn't see him approaching the intersection and took a left turn. He hit her SUV, landed on the road and slid for 60 feet. He was hit around 3:30 a.m. Then it struck me; I wasn't crying over my ex-boyfriend "The Sweet Boy", who has the same name as my brother, I was crying over my brother. It was almost as if I felt him get hit. I immediately knew something was wrong with a Paul.

Although I don't have a romantic love with my brother because that would be fucking weird, I still felt him get hit because I have a genuine love for him. He is a part of me and when he was struck, I was equally struck because love transcends all planes of existence. The point here is that love is very powerful, and we can't keep using what we think is love as a substitute for our inner issues.

Love is real and soulmates do exist, but it's against our nature to believe in such fairy tales.

17. THE DIFFERENCE BETWEEN STANDARD AND LEGENDARY RELATIONSHIPS

So what can we expect a relationship with our soulmate to be like? We can't just look for the basic signs of the standard relationships, such as looks, economic status, build and personality. A legendary relationship has the aforementioned basics along with communication, compromise, understanding, sexual compatibility, stimulating conversations, and support. I will state that sometimes these qualities are mixed. You may get some legendary qualities in your standard relationship. That's a good thing. It means that you're in a relationship that has much to teach you.

Difference between Yelling and Communicating
Standard relationships include a lot of yelling. We get drunk and yell at our partners for flirting with someone, even if they weren't flirting. We fight over what to eat. We fight over the pets. The point is that there isn't any communication, it's just yelling. We don't yell because we care about what the other person is thinking or feeling. We yell because we want to be heard. Yelling is not communication.

Legendary relationships include communication. We have conversations about what's upsetting us. We tell our partners that we feel hurt and they try to understand our point. That goes both ways. If you hurt your partner, you need to listen to what you did and why it bothered them. But communication isn't just confronting issues. We often forget to tell our partners that we love them. Legendary lovers compliment each other frequently.

Legendary lovers express their love more often than standard lovers. That's part of what makes the legendary relationships with our soulmate so desirable. We know that we're appreciated and they know that we appreciate them.

Your legendary relationship is so desirable because you and your soulmate compromise, not settle.

Difference between Settling and Compromise

Settling is when you simply accept the fact that your partner doesn't like what you do and they won't budge on the matter. Instead of breaking it off, you settle because who else is going to love you, right? If your partner doesn't like you watching football with the boys, then you're forced to sacrifice something that you enjoy for the sake of an incompatible partner. If you like having a few drinks with dinner, but your partner hates that you have a glass with each meal, you stop drinking at dinner to pacify them. That's settling.

Legendary lovers understand that their partner won't see eye-to-eye on every factor. However, they will compromise. Compromise is when you and your partner can meet in the middle on something. Let's say you love football and your partner loves hockey. Instead of choosing one to enjoy, you watch both sports together. You support your partner's team and they support yours. My ex-boyfriend didn't care for football because he was a hockey fan, and instead of him trying to stop me from watching the Broncos game or me preventing him for watching the Sharks game, we watched our teams together. That's what we call a compromise.

Understanding

They say that when you meet your soulmate, they can understand your thoughts without you saying a word. Understanding comes from maturity. You either want to understand another person or you don't. That's really what understanding comes down to, personal will. But my best guess is that legendary relationships contain that understanding that comes from really knowing your partner. This is the vibe connection. This happens when you look into their eyes and you see their soul. Understanding also comes from life experience. Either way, your soulmate understands you, and willingly. And more than anything, your soulmate understands your sexual desires.

Sexual Compatibility

Our soulmates don't think our sexual desires are weird, they like them. Some of us like boring sex and others like it rough. It all depends on who you are as a person. You're in a standard relationship if you're submissive and you're partner is uneasy about control. You're in a legendary relationship if you like being dominated and your man loves to dominate you. Some of us like some really weird shit. Well guess what everybody! There's someone out there that loves all of that weird shit you love. That could be your soulmate. But remember! It's not just the sex that makes it your soulmate.

Stimulating Conversations

This concept is pretty straight forward. If you're partner has nothing interesting to say, then you're in a standard relationship. Your legendary relationship is with a person who intrigues you and can hold a conversation about the topics you both enjoy. Like ghosts and UFOs? Your soulmate will, too, or they will at least support the fact that you like ghosts and UFOs.

Support
Your soulmate doesn't laugh at your dreams and goals. Soulmates support each other. They don't just approve of an idea; they embark on that journey together. Not saying that if a woman wants to open a jewelry store that her soulmate has to work there, but her soulmate will be a part of that process. Her partner will be there to see how her business is going. Hell, maybe her soulmate will even help her run the business. The point is that your soulmate doesn't just accept your dreams; they want to fulfill your dreams with you.

Too often we find ourselves in relationships where one person doesn't want to compromise, so we just accept that what we enjoy bothers them. Instead of breaking it off and waiting for the person that completes us, we stay with this energy vampire. If your partner doesn't enjoy you having a few beers and they try to stop you from doing so, you're with the wrong person.

You shouldn't stay with someone that believes that they can control you and fix you. You can't be with someone that wants to change you to what they want you to be. They don't love you for who you are. They are with you because they think they can make you into something that you aren't. That's not a relationship. That is servitude. If you love hiking, you're not going to date someone who hates hiking. The same goes for everything else. There needs to be a compromise. What's worse are the people that believe that they should be chosen over their partner's pet. Ridiculous! I had one guy tell me that I loved Rosie (my beautiful grandma kitty) more than him. I said "no shit" and kicked him out of my house. But maybe that's because I'm a hopeless romantic and I strongly believe that I will find my dream man to protect me.

18. OUR SOULMATE IS OUT THERE

Although most of us have accepted the fact that our perfect someone doesn't exist, I know that everyone at least has a sliver of hope that their soulmate is real.

There are numerous articles out there telling you to give up on finding the perfect person. They want you to just accept the fact that the perfect person doesn't exist. Now, the perfect person may not exist, but your perfect person does. It's all about syntax here. The perfect person implies that you are looking for what society considers perfect. Therefore, they must be a supermodel. But that may not be what is perfect for you.[7]

> By mentally selecting for height, body type, social status, specific skills and interests, intellect, domestic ability and financial status, what we're really doing is deciding that pretty much everyone isn't quite good enough for us. It's time to forget about this perfect person, because they don't exist.

But the perfect someone does exist. You shouldn't just settle for your best friend. That person is your best friend, but probably not your soulmate. Your soulmate is your best friend. I have been tricked into dating a good friend. I was told that I should date this guy because *"he is nice and there aren't a lot of nice guys out there."* So I dated this guy. We got along fine. We would have intelligent conversations. We would enjoy each other's company, but I wasn't sexually attracted to him. I broke up with him. He was upset, but I couldn't believe that I got tricked into dating a guy just because he was nice.

You want a nice guy, by the way. I know that girls love jerks and boys love bitches. That changes as you mature. You realize that jerks are just jerks and bitches are just bitches. Neither a jerk nor a bitch is your soulmate, unless you're one yourself.

The Cosmic Order

And then there's the belief that all of this is written in the stars. Some people, like myself, don't believe in coincidences. I believe that they are signs trying to point us in a direction. But most of us assume that coincidences are just that. There are no divine reasons behind what happens to us, there are just coincidences. This is one, and the most common, way to think. But I believe that we don't notice signs because we're too distracted. But if you believe in soulmates, then you believe in a cosmic order, to some degree.

We all heard the theory that energy cannot be created nor destroyed. We are humans and we are energy. We have the ability to create the realities that we desire. We just need to put some effort in to it.

The cosmic order has your soulmate waiting for you. But if you're one of those people that want to find them so badly that you're constantly looking, you're never going to find them. The universe has the path set for us, and we're always being guided, we just don't listen. We can't focus on trying to find a partner. We must focus on living our lives so that we're led to our soulmate. There is no such thing as being too late. Everything happens as it should, if we listen.

But if we don't listen and we keep seeking out our soulmate, then we're never going to find them. You can't force a soulmate connection. You must embrace life and let it lead you to your soulmate. The cosmic order already knows when you'll meet this person. Consistently looking for your soulmate throws a wrench in the cosmic order. The universe is leading us down this path for a specific reason. We should listen.

The Perfect Person Does Exist

We all have the idea of the perfect person. Just because people tell you that it's impossible to find the perfect person, that doesn't mean they're right. Just because you associate yourself with some Negative Nancys doesn't mean they're speaking words of wisdom.

I know that my perfect man is tall, handsome, protective, funny, intelligent, confident, dominant and respectful. He is a true gentleman. He's financially and mentally stable (I had a thing for crazy dudes for a few minutes there.) And if I'm super lucky, he'll have an accent (domestic or European works for me). Aside from the basics, he will have the qualities of a man in a legendary relationship.

I know that this man exists. Granted, they only made a few of these men and only some are left roaming the planet. I hope to snag one of the remaining few. I choose to have hope. I choose to believe that if I continue to listen to the pings, then I will find my soulmate. There is a perfect person for every person. Don't give up hope and settle. Choose to live the life you were meant to live and enjoy your bliss at the end of the journey.

Your soulmate could be anywhere in this vast world. Listen to your intuition and life will lead you there.

ENDNOTES

1. Romano, Elyse (2014, May 30) *The Biggest Online Dating Services, By The Numbers*. Retrieved from http://www. datingsitesreviews.com/article.php?story=the-biggest-online-dating-services--by-the-numbers

2. Pulley, Anna (2015, May 27) *4 Reasons Humans Are So Bad at Sexual Monogamy*. Retrieved from www.alternet. org/4-reasons-humans-are-so-bad-sexual-monogamy

3. Haven, Chris (2014, February 24) *6 Reasons to Cheat on Your Girlfriend*. Retrieved from http://thoughtcatalog. com/chris-haven/2014/02/6-reasons-to-cheat-on-your-girlfriend/

4. Reinacher, Chris (2014, November 13). *The Terrifying Truth About Being Single*. Retrieved from http://www. buzzfeed.com/chrisreinacher/this-video-proves-why-you-should-stay-with-your-girlfriend#.el730Pnqe

5. Divorce Source. Retrieved from http://www. divorcesource.com/ds/main/u-s-divorce-rates-and-statistics-1037.shtml

6. Divorce Source. Retrieved from http://www. divorcesource.com/ds/main/u-s-divorce-rates-and-statistics-1037.shtml

7. *Forget that perfect person, they don't exist*. Retrieved from http://blog.findsomeone.co.nz/2014/12/19/forget-that-perfect-person-they-dont-exist

ACKNOWLEDGEMENTS

I am beyond thankful to my family for being the best family in the world. Dad and Mom, hopefully, your retirement fund will arrive shortly. I would also like to thank Robin Wilson for all of her help with this book. I couldn't have done it without her.

I want to thank Krystin Borucki for being amazing! Ever since we met, about six years ago, she has always supported me with every wild dream I've ever had. She is my biggest supporter in life, and I love her more every day. I want to thank Dora Orozco for giving me the encouragement to conquer my dreams and Alicia Parrish for being my best friend and life guide for over 12 years.

Thank you to everyone in the Music City Animal Rescue organization. They are the most down to earth people on this planet, and I love them dearly. They are my family here in Tennessee, and I couldn't have done it without them. We will get that shelter built!

Thank you to Will Boyd, Thomas Jackson, and Frank Kramarski for taking the time to review my work. I know that this subject wasn't easy for you all to read about, but you did, and I am beyond grateful. Thank you to Michael Day, my former Professor at Northern Illinois University. He was the first person who saw potential in me and didn't judge me based on my zip code.

Thank you to Ruth Chen for always being amazing. Also a big Thank You to Jeannine East. She is one of the best women on this planet and I love her and her family dearly.

Thank you to my spiritual soul mates Emily Mayberry and Victoria Akpan for reminding me that I am sane even though I think like a cosmic weirdo. Thank you to "The Sweet Boy" for helping me let go of bitterness. He tore down my walls, and it's because of him that I feel free, happy, and finally capable of being loved.

Justin - Hey! Fuck you, buddy!

Thank you to all of the other guys I dated. Even though it never went in a direction that I would have hoped, you all had an impact on my life, and, therefore, a place in this book.

Thank you to my other half. Although I haven't met you yet, I can't wait for us to begin a wonderful life together, with children and all. I know our relationship will be legendary.

Above all, I would like to thank everyone who has ever come into my life, and those who I haven't met yet. I know that all of you have had, or will soon have, a big impact on my life, and it's because of my life experiences and future hope that I am who I am today.

ABOUT THE AUTHOR

Nina Mancuso was born in Rolling Meadows, Illinois and educated at Northern Illinois University. She graduated in 2011 with two degrees, one in English with an emphasis in Rhetoric and Medieval Literature and one in Anthropology with an emphasis in Archaeology. She is currently a technical writer at a software company.

In 2014, she moved down to Nashville, Tennessee to continue growing as a person. Since moving to Nashville, she volunteers her time for Music City Animal Rescue, saving and fostering animals in the Middle Tennessee area.

www.ninaemancuso.com

www.ingramcontent.com/pod-product-compliance
Lightning Source LLC
Chambersburg PA
CBHW061742020426
42331CB00006B/1325